100 Utah Waterfalls

A Preliminary Guide and Survey

by

Dick Wunder

First Printing, August 1999

ISBN 1-891858-08-4

Published by Arch Hunter Books
Thompson Springs, Utah

Prepress by Freedom Industries
Thompson Springs, Utah

Front Cover: Aspen Grove Trail, first waterfall;
Mt. Timpanogos.
Back Cover: Lower Emerald Pool; Zion National Park.

Introduction

"It will be a short book," people said, when my friends told them I was writing a guide to Utah waterfalls. Actually there are many more waterfalls in Utah than anyone imagines. I started with a list of nineteen that I could think of, and my list of possible waterfalls to investigate has grown to ten times that number.

As the subtitle implies, this book is not intended to be definitive. After collecting information for several years I began to realize it was a never-ending project. Whenever I thought I had a complete list as a basis for field work, a new hiking book would mention a waterfall I had never heard of before, or other hikers or staff in a National Forest office would tell me of waterfalls not mentioned in any guidebook.

The publisher and I have therefore decided that the information I have to date would be more useful if published sooner rather than later, so we are issuing this first edition with information as compiled through the end of the 1998 hiking season.

The main text is limited to waterfalls accessible by passenger car and day hiking. For those with 4-wheel drive vehicles and overnight backpacking interests I have included brief information at the end of each section about waterfalls most likely to be worth the extra trouble to visit. Also, I have sometimes included there references to waterfalls whose existence I was not able to verify.

The first part of my research was conducted by reviewing every hiking and driving guide to Utah that I could locate, and making notes of any waterfalls mentioned. I am therefore greatly indebted to all these authors who preceded me, and have included a bibliography of the most useful guidebooks, referring to them in the main text. I recommend the purchase of these guidebooks for further details of the trails I discuss (and for lots of other useful information about Utah).

All of the 100 waterfalls mentioned in the main text have been personally investigated by me, sometimes with hiking companions.

A word about criteria. I have developed no criteria for what constitutes a waterfall, or how high it must be to be included in this book. In general, if a guidebook author thought it worth mentioning I made note of it. If it seemed attractive to me I then included it. Purists who define a waterfall as a perennial drop off of a ledge, or down a rock face, will be unhappy to learn that I have included not only waterfalls and cascades, but notable artificial waterfalls produced by redirection of the natural course of a stream. I have generally included only waterfalls that flow year round; one exception is the frequently photographed spring waterfall at the Temple of Sinawava in Zion National Park.

Directions. Directions to the trailhead are given from the nearest freeway exit or the nearest city. My car has no tenths-of-miles gauge so mileages are approximate.

Trail description. This is intended to be a basic description of the major hiking times between points to give you an idea of how close you are to the waterfall and to keep you in the right direction at junctions or possible places to get lost.

Distances. Three distances are given: driving distance to the trailhead from Salt Lake City (a likely starting point for many people) — this distance is calculated from exit 310 of I-15; driving distance from the nearest city to the trailhead; hiking distance in minutes from the trailhead to the waterfall. I have chosen to give hiking times rather than mileages because I find it a more useful measurement myself and because I would be using it anyway to convert into estimated mileages even if I were using mileages.

Estimated height. Most of these waterfalls have no officially measured height. I've included estimated heights to give you an idea of how much trouble you might want to invest going to a particular waterfall. These heights may be wildly inaccurate; I've discovered in hiking with companions that our estimates vary a lot.

Map and trail guides. This lists the U.S.G.S. 7.5" map on which the waterfall is located and indicates whether it's shown on the map. These maps are sometimes very helpful in orienting yourself, although most Utah waterfalls are not shown on the maps. Whenever appropriate I have listed the trail guides that give the most thorough descriptions of the trails, for those who want more detail than I give in my basic descriptions, or who may want to hike further than just to the waterfall. To save space, I've assigned a four letter code to each guidebook in the bibliography, and use these codes in the main text when I refer to them.

Comments. Other comments may include: whether or not the road is paved all the way to the trailhead; whether you can get to the waterfall without wading boots (by which I mean not the sort of boots used by fishermen, but an old pair of hiking boots that you are willing to use to wade in streams); possible hazards; any other information that seems to me useful or interesting.

Photographs. All photographs, unless otherwise indicated, were taken by me with a small automatic camera, sometimes using the zoom lens.

GNIS. The Geographic Names Information System is a database of named features on U.S. topographical maps, maintained by the U.S. Geological Survey. A search via the internet yielded a list of 24 named "falls" in Utah, about half of which were previously unknown to me. Some of those turned out to be dead ends, some turned out to be river rapids or dryfalls, some do not appear yet on the related maps, but some led to an actual waterfall. I've indicated when my primary information came from the GNIS.

Naming. Most Utah waterfalls have no official name. I've avoided making up names myself, using the name of the canyon or stream to identify them, and using the terms "waterfall" or "cascade" in lower case to indicate that this is not an official name.

General precautions. Always wear hiking boots that cover the ankle; even a paved trail such as Lower Emerald Pool can be slippery or icy. Always carry extra water if hiking any distance. Don't drive on back roads in Utah if rain is threatening. Don't hike in narrow canyons if rain is threatening.

Disclaimer. Hiking is always potentially dangerous, and hiking around the slippery rocks of waterfalls is doubly so. The author and publisher have made a reasonable effort to assess the difficulty of each hike, but make no warranty that the conditions will remain as described, or that you will be free from injury if you use the information in this guidebook. Hike at your own risk.

Reports of other waterfalls. If you know of other waterfalls that you think should have been in this book, please send details to the publisher. We hope to issue an expanded edition in the future.

Arrangement of the book. Waterfalls have been grouped into the following areas of the state:
Northwest Utah (accessed by driving north on I-15)
Salt Lake City Area
Northeast Utah (accessed by driving east on I-80)
Mt. Timpanogos Area
Central Utah (accessed by driving south on I-15)
Southwest Utah (accessed from Cedar City)
Zion National Park
South Central Utah (accessed from Torrey or Escalante)
Southeast Utah (accessed from Moab or Blanding)

About the author. Dick Wunder moved to Utah from Southern California in 1966 and quickly fell in love with the Utah landscape. For more than a quarter century he was Library Director at Westminster College of Salt Lake City before moving to a part time position in the library. He spends much of his spare time driving and hiking throughout the state. As a member of the Natural Arch and Bridge Society he has led hikes at their annual conventions.

Special thanks to Chris Moore, John Remakel, and Joan Reid, companions on the more difficult hikes; to Sandy Pasqua for editorial advice; and to the helpful people in ranger stations and hiking clubs who provided information on lesser known waterfalls.

Dedication

To Dallas A. Forshew, RN, BSN, and Mark B. Bromberg, MD, PhD, the medical team who helped me to recover from a chronic disease and continue hiking.

Contents

(with 7.5" U.S.G.S. maps)

Waterfalls of Northeast Utah

Waterfalls of the Mt. Timpanogos Area

Waterfalls of Northwest Utah

1. Richards Hollow waterfall

p65L *Directions*: From exit 364 of I-15 drive northeast 19 miles on Highway 91. Just past milepost 19, turn east (at the sign for Hardware Ranch) and drive 13 miles on Highway 101, through Hyrum and into Blacksmith Fork toward Hardware Ranch. Just past milepost 13, turn left into Left Hand Fork. Drive up this unpaved road about 4 miles. Just past Friendship Campground, watch for the unmarked trailhead on the left. Park at the trailhead or at pullouts along the road.

Trail description: Follow the trail up the canyon for about 40 minutes until it begins to switchback uphill. There are two short switchbacks, then a long ascent to the waterfall, about 15–20 minutes from the beginning of the switchbacks. The waterfall is just off the trail, downhill to the left.

Distances: 90 mi. from SLC; 12 mi. from Hyrum; 60 min. from trailhead.

Estimated height: 10–15 ft.

Map and trail guide: Logan Peak (not shown); DACA p.32.

Comments: On the east side of Hyrum, Highway 101 jogs one block north before continuing east, although there is no sign to tell you this. The last 4 miles (up Left Hand Fork) are unpaved, poorly maintained, rough and rocky, but passable by passenger car. The trailhead is unmarked, but the trail is wide and obvious. There are three stream crossings, shallow, so wading boots should not be necessary.

2. Ogden Canyon waterfall

Directions: From exit 347 of I-15 drive east about 5 miles on 12th Street (aka Highway 39) to the mouth of Ogden Canyon. Park at milepost 9 just inside the mouth of the canyon. There are small pull-outs on both sides of the highway where the waterfall comes down the north side of the canyon.

Trail description: Roadside.

Distances: 42 mi. from SLC; 2 mi. from Ogden; roadside.

Estimated height: 150 ft., according to Brewer.

Map and trail guide: Ogden (not shown); BRUT p.18.

Comments: This is a beautiful waterfall but not, alas, a natural one; it's a spillway from a water flume. All roads are paved to the waterfall.

Hiked 5/31/14
Steep but amazing!

3. Waterfall Canyon waterfall

Directions: From exit 344A of I-15, drive east about 3 miles to the Mt. Ogden Park Trailhead parking lot at the end of 29th St. A recommended route: continue on 31st St. (as you exit the freeway) to a "dead end" sign; turn left (north) to 30th St.; continue east until 30th ends at St. Benedict Manor; turn left (north) on Polk St. to 29th St.; continue east to the end of 29th St. The parking lot is just to the right.

Trail description: Several well-signed trails depart from the south end of the parking lot. The left-hand one goes to Waterfall Canyon. A broad, easy trail, it climbs uphill to the Bonneville Shoreline Trail, then continues south to the mouth of Waterfall Canyon. Hiking time to this point is about 25 minutes. Waterfall Canyon itself may not be signed; when the Bonneville Trail crosses the stream, stay on the left side of the stream, hiking uphill for about 50 minutes to the foot of the waterfall. This part of the trail is steep and rocky, difficult and difficult to follow. In June the stream overflowed the trail so that I was lured off to the left several times on imaginary bypasses.

Distances: 37 mi. from SLC; 1 mi. from Ogden; 75 min. from the trailhead.

Estimated height: at least 100 ft.

Map and trail guides: Ogden (shown); HAHI p.25–27; DAUT p.32–34, HAHI p.25–27.

Comments: All roads are paved to the trailhead. A trailhead sign calls this Malan Falls, but the name is not used in any guidebooks. A trailhead sign gives the distance to the falls as 1.2 miles, but the steepness of the trail made it seem considerably further, measured by hiking time. When I reached the falls, they were not actually accessible to view, due to the amount of June runoff; standing in the middle of the stream I could see them, but much obscured by trees. Later in the year it may be easier to walk through the stream to the foot of the falls. Wading boots are recommended during spring runoff.

4. Adams Canyon lower waterfall

p65R *Directions*: From exit 326 of I-15 drive north for 6 miles on Highway 89. After passing the signal at Oak Hills Drive, and milepost 340, watch for the next road on the right. Turn here and drive back south along the frontage road to a large parking area where Oak Hills Drive ends at Highway 89.

Trail description: The trail to this waterfall is presently (Spring 1999) being rerouted, so these directions are provisional. Check with the district forest service office if it's not clear where you should go. From the northeast corner of the parking area, walk around the north side of the fence enclosing a small reservoir. Freshly constructed switchbacks lead uphill from here; hike up these switchbacks for about 15 minutes until you reach a level trail heading in both directions along the mountain. Turn right to head into the canyon and continue for about 5 more minutes until you see a connecting trail heading steeply downhill in the opposite direction toward some projecting rocks. (They overlook the canyon above the waterfall.) Head down this trail for about 5 minutes past the rocks to a more level section. Then head downhill again in the opposite direction to the foot of the waterfall. There are a number of alternate trails here; stick with the widest ones and carefully watch your footing on the loose rocks.

Distances: 23 mi. from SLC; 3 mi. from Layton; 15 min. from trailhead.

Estimated height: 20 ft.

Map and trail guide: Kaysville (not shown); word of mouth.

Comments: All roads are paved to the trailhead. Rattlesnakes have been seen on this trail (but it is heavily used by families with children). A sign at the trailhead warns of car break-ins.

5. Adams Canyon cascades

Directions: Follow the directions for No. 4.

Trail description: Follow the directions for No. 4, but when you reach the side trail heading downhill to the lower waterfall, continue on into the canyon. For about 15 minutes the trail is out in the sun; just after entering the trees of the canyon, you will see a side trail leading downhill to a sturdy bridge that crosses the stream. Do not cross this bridge; continue up the canyon on the trail on the north side of the stream. In about 45 minutes cross a plank bridge to the south side of the stream. There are open campsites here, and the cascades, including several small waterfalls, begin here. From this point on the trail is steeper and harder to follow. In some places there are alternate trails; it is usually easier to stay along the bank of the stream when possible. The cascades continue all the way to the upper falls (see No. 6).

Distances: 23 mi. from SLC; 3 mi. from Layton; 80 min. from trailhead.

Estimated height: Various up to 10 ft.

Map and trail guide: Kaysville (not shown); word of mouth.

Comments: See comments for No. 4.

6. Adams Canyon upper waterfall

p66L *Directions*: Follow the directions for No. 4.

Trail description: Follow the same directions as for No. 4 and No. 5. From the second bridge, continue up the trail for another 45 minutes. Just before you reach the waterfall, your way will be blocked by a large rock outcropping; cross the stream to an open hillside of loose rocks. The falls come into view in their alcove as soon as you do this.

Distances: 23 mi. from SLC; 3 mi. from Layton; 2 hours from the trailhead.

Estimated height: 30–35 ft.

Map and trail guide: Kaysville (not shown); word of mouth.

Comments: See the comments for No. 4. The upper portion of this trail is unpleasantly steep, crossing cliffs and loose rocks. But the falls are beautiful. The only place you are likely to need wading boots is the stream crossing just before the falls.

7. Farmington Canyon upper waterfall

Directions: From exit 325 of I-15, drive north and east on Highway 227 to Main St. in Farmington. Drive north on Main St. and then east for one block on 600 North. Turn left on 100 East, which immediately becomes Skyline Drive. Continue up the canyon for 5 miles on this narrow, winding road to Sunset Campground. To avoid paying a day use fee, park in the large area just past the turnoff to the campground.

Trail description: Walk back down the road and into the campground. Follow the road to the trailhead (marked with a small "trail" sign) at the lower end of the campground. Continue down this moderately steep trail for about 10 minutes to where it comes within sound of the stream and then turns downstream. In about 2 minutes the trail comes to a viewpoint where the falls can be seen below the trail. The view is unfortunately blocked by a large tree. Although erosion shows where hikers have climbed down the dangerously steep banks to the foot of the falls, I recommend that they be viewed from the trail.

Distances: 21 mi. from SLC; 6 mi. from Farmington; 20 min. from trailhead.

Estimated height: 25 ft.

Map and trail guide: Peterson (not shown); BUAL p.60–62.

Comments: The last 4 miles of the road are a good quality gravel road, although narrow and heavily traveled.

8. Farmington Canyon lower waterfall

Directions: Follow the directions for No. 7.

Trail description: From No. 7, continue another 5 minutes downstream along the trail. Watch for a steep side trail where you can scramble down through the trees. The falls can be seen only from the stream level. You may have to try a couple of likely places before finding the right one.

Distances: 21 mi. from SLC; 6 mi. from Farmington; 30 min. from trailhead.

Estimated height: 5 ft.

Map and trail guide: Peterson (not shown); BUAL p.60–62.

Comments: See the comments for No. 7.

9. Halfway Creek waterfall

Directions: Follow the directions for No. 7, but watch for a narrow bridge across a side stream, about one mile before Sunset Campground. Park in a small pullout a few hundred feet before the bridge.

Trail description: Walk along the road toward the bridge, and look down at the waterfall below the bridge.

Distances: 20 mi. from SLC; 5 mi. from Farmington; 1 min. from parking pullout.

Estimated height: 15–20 ft.

Map and trail guide: Peterson (not shown); found by serendipity.

Comments: The last 3 miles of the road are a good quality gravel road, although narrow and heavily traveled. There is no trail down to the waterfall.

Other waterfalls of the area: The Burtons (BUAL p.72–73) mention a 20-ft. waterfall in Bair Canyon. I was unable to locate it; other hikers on the trail said there was no waterfall in this canyon, and referred me to Adams Canyon (cf. above) where I found the beautiful waterfalls described above. A hiker told me there were waterfalls in a canyon out of Centerville, but enquiries at city hall and the police department yielded no one who knew of such waterfalls or of a trailhead. There are waterfalls in Willard Canyon that can be seen from a distance.

Waterfalls of the Salt Lake City Area

10. Church Fork upper waterfall

p66R *Directions*: From exit 128 of I-80, drive south on I-215 for 2 miles to exit 3. Turn left to Wasatch Blvd. and drive south 5 blocks to 38th South. Turn left (east) into Mill Creek Canyon. Drive 3 miles to Church Fork Picnic Area on the left. Drive to the parking area for hikers at the top of the picnic area, or park along the road outside the picnic area.

Trail description: The Church Fork stream flows down through the picnic area, creating several cascading waterfalls along the way. This one is up the trail about one minute above the parking area.

Distances: 12 mi. from SLC; 1 min. from trailhead.

Estimated height: 15 ft.

Map and trail guide: Mount Aire (not shown); word of mouth.

Comments: The road is paved all the way to the trailhead. A fee is charged for entering Mill Creek Canyon. There are several other cascades and waterfalls along the road as the stream cascades down through the picnic area.

11. Church Fork roadside waterfall

Directions: Follow the directions for No. 10.

Trail description: From the parking area walk back down the road about halfway to the entrance to the picnic area. This waterfall is beside the road.

Distances: 12 mi. from SLC; 5 min. from trailhead.

Estimated height: 5 ft.

Map and trail guide: Mount Aire (not shown); word of mouth.

Comments: See the comments for No. 10.

12. Heughes Canyon waterfall

Directions: From exit 301 of I-15, drive east on 7200 South (aka Fort Union Blvd.) for 6 miles to Wasatch Blvd. (the major traffic signal at the mouth of Big Cottonwood Canyon). Turn north and drive for about 2 miles, staying on Wasatch Blvd. as it curves to the right. Turn east onto Canyon Cove Dr. (6250 So.) and then left onto Oak Canyon Dr. (3480 East). Park near the intersection of Oak Canyon and Berghalde Ln. (6145 So.), being careful to stay away from private driveways.

Trail description: Hike up Berghalde Ln. (a private road open only to hikers entering the national forest) for about 10 minutes to the mouth of the canyon. The trail

continues up canyon on the north side of the stream. In about 30 minutes a side trail takes off on the left; continue beside the stream. In another 5 minutes the trail crosses to the south side of the stream and in about 15 minutes crosses back again. A steep climb uphill for 5–10 minutes leads to a rock fall that the trail crosses. A large rock part way across the rock fall gives the best view of the falls, which is in a cleft on the south side of the canyon.

Distances: 17 mi. from SLC; 70 min. from the trailhead.

Estimated height: 30–40 ft.

Map and trail guide: Sugar House (not shown); information from a member of the Wasatch Mountain Club.

Comments: All roads are paved to the trailhead. This trail has recently been released from private ownership for public hiking; be careful not to annoy private homeowners along the way, to ensure continued access. The foot of the falls can be accessed by clambering along the loose rocks at the base of the rock slide. There are logs across the stream at both crossings, so wading boots should not be necessary. There are smaller falls and cascades along the stream on the way up.

13. Lake Blanche outlet waterfall

p67L *Directions*: From exit 301 of I-15 drive east on 7200 South (aka Fort Union Blvd.) for 6 miles to the mouth of Big Cottonwood Canyon. Continue up the canyon for about 5 miles to the “S” curve just past milepost 6. Park in the parking area just off the road at the bottom of the “S” curve, or in the small parking area in the middle of the “S” curve.

Trail description: From the parking area continue east along the paved side road to the outlet of the stream from Lake Blanche.

Distances: 20 mi. from SLC; 5 min. from trailhead.

Estimated height: 10 ft.

Map and trail guide: Mount Aire (not shown); HAHI p.42–45.

Comments: All roads are paved to the trailhead. There are other waterfalls at the outlets of Lakes Blanche and Florence. Winter set in before I was able to do field work to include them in this book.

14. Hidden Falls

p67R *Directions*: Follow the directions for No. 13.

Trail description: Climb the steps on the north side of the parking area in the middle of the “S” curve and cross the highway to the trailhead for Mill B North Fork.

Instead of following the trail up the hill to the right, continue directly ahead up the stream. Hidden Falls is a short way up stream.

Distances: 20 mi. from SLC; 3 min. from trailhead.

Estimated height: 10–15 ft.

Map and trail guide: Mount Aire (shown); HAHI p.39–41, VEHI p.100, NITR p.66.

Comments: All roads are paved to the trailhead. You can walk up either side of the stream without wading boots. This is the shortest hike to a Utah waterfall, aside from those that are visible from the road.

15. Moss Ledge

Directions: Follow the directions for No. 13, continuing another mile to the small parking area at Moss Ledge picnic area on the left, just at milepost 7.

Trail description: Hike up through the picnic area for about 5 minutes to the last table on the left side of the stream. The stream comes down over the rocks as a waterfall into the picnic area.

Distances: 21 mi. from SLC; 5 min. from trailhead.

Estimated height: 30 ft. cascade.

Map and trail guide: Mount Aire (not shown); information from a member of the Wasatch Mountain Club.

Comments: Another waterfall comes down from the picnic area at the parking area, but vanishes beneath the rocks by late summer.

16. Mineral Fork cascade

Directions: Follow the directions for No. 13, continuing another 2 miles to the trailhead just before milepost 8. Watch for the "fill" bridge across the stream on the right. The trailhead is unmarked, except for a small sign across the bridge. There are small parking areas along the highway and across the bridge.

Trail description: The trail is an old jeep road (now blocked by rock falls) leading up to abandoned mines. About 15–20 minutes from the trailhead, a large cascade comes down over the road from the left. The trail immediately switch-

backs and crosses the cascade a second time.

Distances: 22 mi. from SLC; 15 min. from trailhead.

Estimated height: 40 ft.

Map and trail guide: Mount Aire (not shown); no guide.

Comments: All roads are paved to the trailhead. Bottcher (BOWA p.41) mentions waterfalls "from the high cirque" but not this cascade. There are no other waterfalls evident between here and the mines below the cirque, and when I explored the trail in late July there were no waterfalls coming from the cirque; they are apparently fed by snowmelt and are not perennial.

17. Laurel Pines spring

Directions: Follow the directions for No. 13, continuing another 4 miles to just before milepost 10; the spring in the form of a waterfall is right beside the road on the left, across the highway from the entrance to a private area signed "Laurel Pines."

Trail description: Roadside.

Distances: 24 mi. from SLC; roadside.

Estimated height: 5 ft.

Map and trail guide: Mount Aire (not shown); found by serendipity.

Comments: All roads are paved to the trailhead. An attractive falls in spite of its exposed roadside location.

18. Doughnut Falls

p68L *Directions*: Follow the directions for No. 13, continuing another 5 miles to the entrance road to Cardiff Fork, just before milepost 11. Drive up the road about a mile, past the Jordan Pines campground, to a small parking area where the road turns to the right and crosses the stream as a jeep road.

Trail description: A small trailhead sign is at the south end of the parking lot. Follow this trail (an old jeep road) uphill for about 7 minutes until it leaves the old road as a trail on the right. In another 7 minutes it crosses a bridge and rejoins the main jeep road that crossed the stream back at the parking area. Continue up this road for another 7 minutes, keeping left at the "Y," until it comes to a small rock outcropping. Climb down the rocks and continue upstream for a few minutes to a view of the falls. The water falls through a hole in the roof of a cave (forming an arch) and then cascades steeply downstream. Some people — including small children — climb up the boulders into the cave but I considered them too slippery. The best route seems to be to climb up the right side of the stream. If you decide to do this, you'll want wading boots.

Distances: 25 mi. from SLC; 25 min. from trailhead.

Estimated height: 15 ft. plus cascades.

Map and trail guide: Mount Aire (shown); NITR p.70, VEHI p.112.

Comments: All roads are paved to the trailhead. Although sometimes listed as Donut Falls, Doughnut Falls is the official name in the GNIS.

19. Silver Fork waterfall

Directions: Follow the directions for No. 13, continuing another 8 miles to the entrance to the Solitude Ski Resort, just past milepost 14. Park outside the gate, which is locked in summer. Be careful not to block the gate, which gives access to private homes in Silver Fork.

Trail description: From the northwest corner of the parking lot, follow the road which passes below the Inspiration and Eagle Express ski lifts and winds above the private cabins in Silver Fork. In about 15 minutes the pavement ends as the road turns the corner at the Silver Hill lodge and continues south into the National Forest. In another 5 minutes you will come to a locked gate across the road; in another 10 minutes to an RV under a shed, at the junction into Honeycomb Fork. Continue to the right and begin watching for the waterfall down in the stream to the left. You should reach it in 4 or 5 minutes.

Distances: 28 mi. from SLC; 35 min. from trailhead.

Estimated height: 10 ft.

Map and trail guide: Brighton (not shown); VEHI p.119–121 mentions "small waterfalls" further on in upper Silver Fork, but not this one.

Comments: All roads are paved to the trailhead. Most of the land along the lower sections of the road is privately owned; be careful not to trespass off the road. There is no trail down to the waterfall. The weather conspired to keep me from exploring for the other waterfalls.

Little Cottonwood Canyon Waterfalls

Most of these falls (Nos. 20–29) can be viewed only from a distance as they descend the steep cliffs or stream beds of the southern subsidiary streams flowing into Little Cottonwood Creek. They are most easily located when driving down canyon, although the mileage markers are not numbered on the downhill side. To reach Little Cottonwood Canyon: from exit 301 of I-15, drive east on 7200 South (aka Fort Union Blvd.) for 6 miles to the mouth of Big Cottonwood Canyon. At the traffic signal at the mouth of the canyon, turn right (south) onto Highway 210. This highway continues around the foothills and into Little Cottonwood Canyon. The highway is paved to all of these waterfalls.

20. Thunder Mountain waterfall

Directions: Follow the general directions above. Between mileposts 5 and 6, watch for the power plant (a small square building) at the end of a good-sized parking area. Park here.

Trail descriptions: From the middle of the parking area, look through gaps in the trees for the waterfall in the cliffs high above you, and slightly up canyon.

Distances: 20 mi. from SLC; roadside.

Estimated height: 100 ft.

Map and trail guide: Dromedary Peak (not shown); mentioned briefly in MANF p.98 and VEHI p.136.

Comments: Hike up and down canyon along the highway, looking up through breaks in the trees for additional views. My designation for this falls is a guess based on examining the topo map.

21. Coalpit Gulch waterfall

Directions: Follow the directions for No. 20.

Trail description: From the power plant parking area, walk up the highway for about 10 minutes, watching through breaks in the trees. There are good views just before milepost 6.

Distances: 20 mi. from SLC; roadside.

Estimated height: 100 ft.

Map and trail guide: Dromedary Peak (not shown); mentioned briefly in MANF p.98 and VEHI p.136.

Comments: Veranth (VEHI p.190) mentions 3 waterfalls in Coalpit Gulch accessible to groups with rock climbing experience.

22. Lisa Falls

Directions: Continue up canyon from the previous parking spot. The parking area for Lisa Falls is on the left (north) between mileposts 6 and 7. The trail is unmarked but there are usually cars parked there to alert you.

Trail description: Walk up the trail for about 5–10 minutes to a view of the falls pouring down over a large slab of rock in an open area.

Distances: 21 mi. from SLC; 5 min. from trailhead.

Estimated height: 20 ft.

Map and trail guide: Dromedary Peak (not shown); information from GNIS

and from Wasatch Mountain Club hiking map.

Comments: The name is from the GNIS.

23. Hogum Fork waterfall

Directions: Continue up canyon from the previous parking area. Park near milepost 7.

Trail description: Walk up and down canyon along the highway for views of this waterfall on the south side of the canyon.

Distances: 22 mi. from SLC; roadside.

Estimated height: 100 ft.

Map and trail guide: Dromedary Peak (not shown); mentioned briefly in MANF p.98 and VEHI p.136.

Comments: You may need to drive back and forth a few times to distinguish this waterfall from the one in Maybird Gulch (No. 24).

24. Maybird Gulch waterfall

Directions: Continue up canyon for a short way and park between milepost 7 and 8.

Trail description: Walk up and down canyon along the highway for views of this waterfall on the south side of the canyon.

Distances: 22 mi. from SLC; roadside.

Estimated height: 150 ft.

Map and trail guide: Dromedary Peak (not shown); mentioned briefly in MANF p.98 and VEHI p.136; cf. also VEHI p.139–40 for a mention of a waterfall that appears to be further upstream.

Comments: This is more difficult to spot than some of the others; views of it are blocked by roadside trees when driving up canyon. It is very close to Hogum Fork; the two canyons are on two sides of a rounded mound. The flow of water in Maybird Gulch is narrow and less than the others.

25. Red Pine Fork waterfall

Directions: Continue up canyon to the lower end of the Tanner Flat Slide Area, just at milepost 8, within sight of the Tanner Flat Campground.

Trail description: There is a good view of this falls at this point.

Distances: 23 mi. from SLC; roadside.

Estimated height: 70 ft.

Map and trail guide: Dromedary Peak (not shown); mentioned briefly in MANF p.98 and VEHI p.136.

Comments: This is one of the best and closest of the roadside falls in Little Cottonwood Canyon.

26. Tanner Flat Campground waterfall

Directions: Follow the same directions as for No. 25.

Trail description: Walk into the campground and go to campsite #36. From here the waterfall can be seen a short distance upstream. There is no trail to the waterfall; the bank is lined with brush and boulders.

Distances: 23 mi. from SLC; 10 min. from trailhead to view of waterfall.

Estimated height: 5 ft.

Map and trail guide: Dromedary Peak (not shown); word of mouth.

Comments: There is an entrance fee for walking into the campground.

27. White Pine Fork waterfall

Directions: Continue up canyon to the lower end of the parking area at the White Pine Slide Area, just before milepost 9.

Trail description: There is a good view of the falls in this area.

Distances: 24 mi. from SLC; roadside.

Estimated height: 70 ft.

Map and trail guide: Dromedary Peak (not shown); mentioned briefly in MANF p.98 and VEHI p.136.

Comments: As can be seen from the photograph, this waterfall is difficult to see among the trees, especially later in the year.

28. Peruvian Gulch waterfalls

p68R *Directions*: Continue up canyon and park above Cliff Lodge at Snowbird entry 4, near milepost 10.

Trail description: Several waterfalls can be seen in a section of cliffs in the gulch southeast of Cliff Lodge. A bushwhacking trail has been worn to one of the lower falls, but is not recommended. For a view of a 10 ft. falls further up the gulch, drive into Alta, park at the bottom of the road leading to the Blackjack condominiums, and hike up the road for about 30 minutes to a switchback. Look down into the gulch for a view of the falls.

Distances: 25 mi. from SLC; roadside, or 30 min. from trailhead.

Estimated height: Various.

Map and trail guide: Dromedary Peak (not shown); found by serendipity.

Comments: The photo shows the lower falls at the end of the bushwhacking trail. This appears to be different than the one that can be seen from the road above the lodge. It's too bad there is no constructed trail to any of the falls in this gulch.

29. Alta City waterfall

p69L *Directions*: Continue up canyon to the turnoff to the alternate route down through Alta to Cliff Lodge, between milepost 10 and 11. A few hundred yards down the road there is a bridge over Little Cottonwood Creek. Park on the south side of the bridge.

Trail description: Walk to the edge of the parking area and look down into the canyon, downstream of the bridge, for a view of the falls.

Distances: 26 mi. from SLC; roadside.

Estimated height: 20 ft. plus cascades.

Map and trail guide: Dromedary Peak (not shown); found by serendipity.

Comments: A very fine, classic waterfall. Unfortunately there is no trail to the foot of the falls and the cliffs are dangerously steep.

30. Bells Canyon lower waterfall

Directions: From exit 301 of I-15, drive east on 7200 South (aka Fort Union Blvd.) for 6 miles to the mouth of Big Cottonwood Canyon. At the traffic signal at the mouth of the canyon, turn right (south) onto Highway 210. Drive south for 2 miles to the traffic light past milepost 2 and turn right onto Wasatch Blvd. (unsigned). Drive south another 1 or 2 miles through the traffic light at Little Cottonwood Rd. (9800 So.). Turn left at the bottom of the first hill onto Stone Mtn. Lane (10050 So.), and continue into the cul-de-sac, keeping left at all intersections. Just before the intersection of Stone Mtn.

Dr. (sic) and Stone Mesa Ct., park along the fenced yards on the south side of the street, to avoid annoying the residents.

Trail description: From the parking area walk to the end of the cul-de-sac where an old service road leads uphill to the lower reservoir. You should reach the reservoir in 20 minutes. Proceed around the left side of the reservoir and continue uphill for another 10 minutes to an old building (apparently controlling or measuring water flow). From here the route is difficult to describe, since there are many trails going in many directions. The trail forks; the right fork crosses the stream on a metal bridge above the building. But take the left fork and continue for 5 minutes through an oak wood, across the upper end of a swampy meadow, through another oak wood to where the trail you are following joins a well-worn trail coming uphill. Turn right and follow the well-worn trail uphill for 10 minutes until it crosses an open sage flat and reaches the stream again. Cross the stream here on a bridge made of small logs tied together with string. From here a trail continues uphill on the right side of the stream. Follow this for about 60 minutes to the waterfall. This section of the trail is washed out in many places so that it seems as if you are hiking in a dry stream bed; persevere.

Distances: 19 mi. from SLC; 105 min. to waterfall.

Estimated height: 60 ft. cascade.

Map and trail guide: Draper (not shown); NITR p.30–31, GEWA p.27–28, HAHI p.49–54, NITR p.30–31.

Comments: There are other waterfalls higher up, according to the trail guides, which mostly describe the hike as a downhill hike after climbing Lone Peak. Thanks to Sandy City Parks for providing information on trailhead access. For current information on this and other trailheads into this national forest, call Sandy City Parks at 568–2900.

31. Rocky Mouth waterfall

Directions: From exit 301 of I-15, drive east on 7200 South (aka Fort Union Blvd.) for 6 miles to the mouth of Big Cottonwood Canyon. At the traffic signal at the mouth of the canyon, turn right (south) onto Highway 210 and continue for 2 miles. Just past mileage marker 2 turn right (south) at a traffic signal onto Wasatch Drive. Drive south for another 3 miles, watching for an LDS chapel on the right. Just south of this chapel, at approximately 11248 South, there is a small graveled parking lot for six cars, on the left (east) side of the road. Park here.

Trail description: From the northeast corner of the parking lot, climb the wooden stairway up the hill to the residential area above. Turn right onto the sidewalk and continue south. Ahead you will see the mouth of the canyon, just beyond a small covered and fenced reservoir. Walk up the hill and along the trail behind the reservoir to the mouth of the canyon. Proceed up the canyon for a few minutes until you see the waterfall ahead of you through the trees. To reach the foot of the falls it is necessary to climb up a steep hill of loose rocks through the dry stream bed. Footing can be a little treacherous here, but it is not particularly dangerous. The total hiking time from Wasatch Blvd. to the waterfall is about 15 minutes.

Distances: 20 mi. from SLC; 15 min. from trailhead.

Estimated height: 40 ft.

Map and trail guide: Draper (not shown); information from a member of the Wasatch Mountain Club.

Comments: A well-kept secret. Although I've lived in SLC for 30 years I had never heard of this beautiful waterfall before this year. Thanks to Sandy City Parks for providing trailhead parking and information on trailhead access. Please use the parking lot provided rather than parking near the private homes above. For current information on this and other trailheads into this national forest, call Sandy City Parks at 568–2900.

Other waterfalls of the area. Geery (GEWA p.50) mentions cascades in upper Broads Fork. Hall (HAHI p.42–45) mentions waterfalls in the Lake Blanche area. Nichols (NITR p.60) mentions cascades in Stairs Gulch; these are attractive but small.

Waterfalls of Northeast Utah

32. Ely Creek waterfall

p69R *Directions*: From exit 148 of I-80, drive east on Highway 40 through Heber and Duchesne for 145 miles to the center of Vernal. Drive north on Highway 191 to 500 North, then follow the signs east for 40 miles to Jones Hole National Fish Hatchery.

Trail description: From the visitor parking lot, hike down through the fish hatchery and downstream on the relatively level trail for 40 minutes, to where the trail crosses Jones Creek on a bridge. Continue for another 10 minutes to a campsite with a trail heading south, signed "Island Park 8.0 Miles." Hike down this trail for about 5 minutes to the waterfall.

Distances: 218 mi. from SLC; 40 mi. from Vernal; 55 min. from trailhead.

Estimated height: 14 ft.

Map and trail guide: Jones Hole (not shown); HAHI p.118–121.

Comments: All roads are paved to the trailhead, although in poor condition in places. Just across the bridge are rock art panels on the walls behind the bushes; be sure to stop and see them. As long as you've come this far, go on down the main trail for a view of Burnt Springs waterfall.

33. Burnt Springs waterfall

Directions: Follow the same directions as for No. 32.

Trail description: Follow the same directions as for No. 32. At the trail junction 10 minutes past the bridge, continue down the main trail for about 15 minutes. Watch for the thin stream of water from Burnt Springs, falling off the headwall of a small side canyon on the north.

Distances: 218 mi. from SLC; 40 mi. from Vernal; 65 min. from trailhead.

Estimated height: 50 ft.

Map and trail guide: Jones Hole (not shown); information from sign at trailhead.

Comments: It might be possible to bushwhack to a closer view of this falls, but the flow of water is not impressive, and it would be necessary to wade Jones Hole Creek, which is deep and swift and narrow at this point. See also the comments for No. 32.

34. Jones Creek waterfall

Directions: Follow the same directions as for No. 32.

Trail description: Follow the same directions as for No. 33. Watch for a place just opposite the Burnt Springs waterfall, where a rock outcropping along the trail affords a good viewpoint. This small waterfall is in the main stream beside the rock outcropping. Continue on down the trail a few more feet for access to a good view from the bank.

Distances: 218 mi. from SLC; 40 mi. from Vernal; 65 min. from trailhead.

Estimated height: 3 ft.

Map and trail guide: Jones Hole (not shown); found by serendipidy.

Comments: See the comments for No. 32.

35. Big Spring [Sheep Creek]

Directions: From exit 148 of I-80, drive east on Highway 40 through Heber and Duchesne for 145 miles to the center of Vernal. Drive north on Highway 191 for 34 miles (between milepost 235 and 236) to the junction with Highway 44. Drive north on 44 for 22 miles to the entrance to the Sheep Creek Geological Loop (at milepost 22). Drive south along Sheep Creek for 6 miles to Big Spring (signed), which cascades out of the foot of a cliff into Sheep Creek, across the creek from the highway pullout.

Trail description: Roadside.

Distances: 240 mi. from SLC; 62 mi. from Vernal; roadside.

Estimated height: 10 ft.

Map and trail guide: Jessen Butte (shown); information from roadside sign; MANA p.97 gives a highway description but does not mention the spring.

Comments: All roads are paved. A recreation pass is required to drive and park in the Flaming Gorge area.

36. Smooth Rock Falls

p70L *Directions*: From exit 148 of I-80 drive southeast 4 miles on Highway 40 to Highway 248. Drive east 12 miles to Kamas. In Kamas, turn north to the intersection of Main and Center, then east on Highway 150. Drive to milepost 20, where there is a small pullout, then stop at the next pullout (unsigned), which looks like the entrance to a side road. The "falls" are a series of small cascades in the river beside the road.

Trail description: Walk down beside the river for a view of one cascade just upstream from the viewpoint, and another just downstream.

Distances: 69 mi. from SLC; 20 mi. from Kamas; roadside.

Estimated height: 3 ft.

Map and trail guide: Iron Mine Mountain (not shown); information from GNIS and maps.

Comments: This is not a particularly remarkable cascade, and is included only because it is easy to get to and is a named feature on topographic maps. A recreation pass is required to drive and park in this area.

37. Slate Gorge lower waterfall

Directions: Follow the same directions as for No. 36. Continue 2 miles to the Slate Gorge Overlook between mileposts 22 and 23. The overlook is not signed ahead of time and is a little difficult to see until you are almost there.

Trail description: Walk downhill behind the outhouse for a view of the falls down in the gorge.

Distances: 71 mi. from SLC; 22 mi. from Kamas; 1 min. from trailhead to view of falls (or 20 min. from trailhead to foot of falls, using directions below).

Estimated height: 40 ft.

Map and trail guide: Mirror Lake (not shown); found by serendipity.

Comments: To reach the bottom of the falls, drive back to milepost 22, where there are several roads going in different directions. Take the furthest left hand road to where it ends in a large circular parking area. At the

north end of the parking area you will find a steep fisherman's trail going downhill to the river. From there you can walk upstream for about 20 minutes to a spot where you can see around the corner to the falls. You may have to cross the river a couple of times to avoid a place where it comes up against the cliffs; wading boots are recommended and caution is needed, since the rocks in the river are smooth and slimy. At one point there are stair step cascades similar to those pictured as Archangel Cascades in Zion National Park. A recreation pass is required to drive and park in this area.

38. Slate Gorge middle waterfall

Directions: Follow the same directions as for No. 37.

Trail description: Walk up a short trail at the north end of the parking lot for a view of this waterfall down in the gorge.

Distances: 71 mi. from SLC; 22 mi. from Kamas; 1 min. from trailhead.

Estimated height: 10 ft.

Map and trail guide: Mirror Lake (not shown); found by serendipity.

Comments: A recreation pass is required to drive and park in this area.

(Upper photo: 38. Slate Gorge middle waterfall.)

39. Slate Gorge upper waterfall

Directions: Follow the same directions as for No. 37.

Trail description: Walk up a short trail at the north end of the parking lot for a view of this waterfall upstream in the gorge, before the next bend to the left.

Distances: 71 mi. from SLC; 22 mi. from Kamas; 1 min. from trailhead.

Estimated height: 50 ft.

Map and trail guide: Mirror Lake (not shown); found by serendipity.

Comments: A recreation pass is required to drive and park in this area.

40. Slate Gorge side canyon waterfall

Directions: Follow the same directions as for No. 37.

Trail description: From the parking lot walk up the highway for 5 minutes to where a side stream flows through a culvert. On the far side of the bridge, walk down into the forest on the right. Continue downhill for 5–10 minutes, staying back from the cliff edge, until you see a point ahead of you overlooking the gorge. Walk down to this point, from which you can look downstream to where the side stream drops in a waterfall into Slate Gorge. There is no trail to bring you closer to the waterfall.

Distances: 71 mi. from SLC; 22 mi. from Kamas; 15 min. from trailhead.

Estimated height: 30 ft.

Map and trail guide: Mirror Lake (not shown); found by serendipity.

Comments: A recreation pass is required to drive and park in this area.

41. Provo River Falls upper waterfall

p70R *Directions*: Follow the same directions as for No. 37. Continue another mile to the parking lot on the left just before milepost 24.

Trail description: A partly paved trail leads out to the first waterfall, and then downstream for a few yards to the other two major falls.

Distances: 73 mi. from SLC; 24 mi. from Kamas; 2 min. from the trailhead.

Estimated height: 20 ft.

Map and trail guide: Mirror Lake (shown); BESC p.169–73.

Comments: All roads are paved to the trailhead. A recreation pass is required to drive and park in this area.

42. Provo River Falls middle waterfall

p71L *Directions*: Follow the same directions as for No. 41.

Trail description: Walk downstream for 1–2 minutes to the middle falls.

Distances: 73 mi. from SLC; 24 mi. from Kamas; 4 min. from the trailhead.

Estimated height: 15 ft.

Map and trail guide: Mirror Lake (shown); BESC p.169–173.

Comments: See the comments for No. 41.

43. Provo River Falls lower waterfall

p71R *Directions*: Follow the same directions as for No. 41.

Trail description: Walk downstream a few more minutes to the lower falls.

Distances: 73 mi. from SLC; 24 mi. from Kamas; 7 min. from trailhead.

Estimated height: 20 ft.

Map and trail guide: Mirror Lake (shown); BESC p.169–173.

Comments: See the comments for No. 41.

44. Ostler Creek cascades

Directions: From exit 148 of I-80 drive southeast 4 miles on Highway 40 to Highway 248. Drive east 12 miles to Kamas. In Kamas, turn north to the intersection of Main and Center, then east on Highway 150. Drive 45 miles, past Mirror Lake, to the turnoff to Christmas Meadows between mileposts 45 and 46 (just past the turnoff to Stillwater Campground). Drive 4 miles to the parking area at the Christmas Meadows trailhead.

Trail description: Hike south on the trail down the Stillwater River valley. In about 70 minutes the trail moves close to the Stillwater River and continues beside it. In another 10 minutes you should come to the Uinta Wilderness boundary sign, and in another 5 minutes to a junction. The junction is easy to miss; it is marked only with a small sign on a tree. Straight ahead the trail continues to Kermsuh and Ryder lakes. Turn left toward Amethyst Lake. In about 5 minutes the trail begins to climb steeply beside the cascades of Ostler Creek. The cascades continue for about 15–20 minutes in varied waterfalls beside the trail.

Distances: 98 mi. from SLC; 50 mi. from Kamas; 90 min. from the trailhead.

Estimated height: many cascades, up to 50 ft.

Map and trail guide: Christmas Meadows (not shown); DAUT p.49–51.

Comments: The last 4 miles to the trailhead are unpaved. There are many side streams and boggy spots across the trail. Stepping stones and log bridges have been provided, so it should not be necessary to wear wading boots. A recreation pass is required to drive and park in this area.

Other waterfalls in this area: The GNIS lists Ashley Falls on the Dutch John topo. This is a falls in Red Canyon of the Green River, which was encountered by William Ashley's fur trapping party when they were exploring in 1825; it is now inundated underneath Flaming Gorge Reservoir. The GNIS also lists Merkley Drop on the Whiterocks 7.5 topo; this is where the water from the Whiterocks and Ouray Valley Canal "drops" down the hill into Ouray Valley on its way to Merkley Reservoir; I was unable to find any public access to a view of this "falls." The Bear River ranger station reports a cascade waterfall (shown on maps of the Uintas), known as Scout Falls, and reached by hiking up the Bear River from the East Fork Bear River BSA Camp. The Kamas ranger station reports waterfalls in Cataract Gorge, accessed by a very rough 4WD road off the Murdoch Basin road. Fall Creek in the Uintas is known to have waterfalls — cf. HAHI p.107–111 — but appears to be too far for day hiking.

Waterfalls of the Mt. Timpanogos Area

45. Dry Creek Canyon waterfall

Directions: From exit 287 of I-15, drive east 5 miles to the traffic signal. Turn left (north) and drive 2 miles to the center of Alpine. At 200 North turn east to 200 East. Drive north on 200 East (which becomes Grove Dr.) for about 2 miles until it becomes a rocky dirt road. Continue on this road around a couple of corners to a large parking area.

Trail description: A trail register above the parking area marks the trailhead. The trail is broad and easy, though steep in places. After about 40 minutes there is a side stream to cross, a second in another 15 minutes, and a third in another 10 minutes. In another 10 minutes a short trail on the left leads to a viewpoint where the waterfall can be seen across the canyon.

Distances: 32 mi. from SLC; 2 mi. from Alpine; 75 min. from the trailhead.

Estimated height: 30 ft.

Map and trail guide: Timpanogos Cave (not shown); information from National Forest Service.

Comments: The last few hundred feet to the trailhead are unpaved. The side streams are fairly shallow so wading boots should not be necessary. It may be possible to bushwhack to a closer view of the falls. On the downstream side of the third stream crossing is a small waterfall worth noting.

46. Battle Creek Canyon first waterfall

p72L *Directions*: From exit 279 of I-15, drive east about a mile to State Street (Highway 89). Turn south and drive about 2 miles, then turn left (at the curve) onto Center St. in Pleasant Grove. In the center of town, turn south to 200 South. Turn east and drive for 2 miles on 200 South (Battle Creek Dr.) to the mouth of the canyon. Park at the Kiwanis Park just past the water tower.

Trail description: From the Kiwanis Park, walk up the canyon for about 10 minutes to the end of the dirt road. (With high clearance you can drive to this point.) Continue on the trail for 3 minutes to the bridge, then up the hill another 3 minutes to a view of the falls. A trail leads down a steep rocky slope to the foot of the falls.

Distances: 36 mi. from SLC; 2 mi. from Pleasant Grove; 15 min. from trailhead.

Estimated height: 30 ft.

Map and trail guide: Orem (not shown); KLCL p.82–84, 87, 94, PAUT p.12.

Comments: All roads are paved to the trailhead. Be sure to continue up the trail to the next two waterfalls.

47. Battle Creek Canyon second waterfall

p72R *Directions*: Follow the same directions as for No. 46.

Trail description: Follow the same directions as for No. 46. Continue up the trail for another 5 minutes to the second waterfall, beside the trail.

Distances: 36 mi. from SLC; 2 mi. from Pleasant Grove; 20 min. from trailhead.

Estimated height: 7 ft.

Map and trail guide: Orem (not shown); found by serendipity.

Comments: All roads are paved to the trailhead.

48. Battle Creek Canyon third waterfall

Directions: Follow the same directions as for No. 46.

Trail description: Follow the same directions as for Nos. 46 and 47. Continue up the trail for another 10 minutes. About 2 minutes after the trail crosses a second bridge, the third waterfall can be seen downhill to the left; the trail climbs steeply beside it.

Distances: 36 mi. from SLC; 2 mi. from Pleasant Grove; 30 min. from trailhead.

Estimated height: 7 ft.

Map and trail guide: Orem (not shown); found by serendipity.

Comments: Besides these three waterfalls, there are smaller cascades all along the stream that are worth noting.

49. Timpooneke Trail first waterfall

Directions: From exit 287 of I-15, drive east 16 miles on Highway 92 (the Alpine Scenic Loop) to the turnoff to the Timpooneke Campground and trailhead parking for the Timpooneke Trail. Drive in about half a mile to the trailhead parking area.

Trail description: The trail climbs

gradually, contouring around the side of the lower valley toward the eastern cliffs. In about 35 minutes you should reach the first waterfall, cascading down across the trail.

Distances: 39 mi. from SLC; 13 mi. from Alpine; 35 min. from trailhead.

Estimated height: 30 ft. down to the trail; another 30 feet below the trail.

Map and trail guide: Timpanogos Cave (not shown); PAUT p.24, DAUT p.140–143, KLCL p.132–136.

Comments: All roads are paved to the trailhead. This trail is heavily used; don't expect to park at the trailhead on a summer weekend. A recreation pass, or a federal pass, is required to enter this area.

50. Timpooneke Trail second waterfall

Directions: Follow the same directions as for No. 49.

Trail description: Continue up the trail from No. 49 for about 5 minutes to this waterfall pouring over mossy stones.

Distances: 39 mi. from SLC; 13 mi. from Alpine; 40 min. from trailhead.

Estimated height: 5 ft.

Map and trail guide: Timpanogos Cave (not shown); PAUT p.24, DAUT p.140–143, KLCL p.132–136.

Comments: Just before reaching this waterfall there is a good view of the right hand side of Scout Falls. See also the comments for No. 49.

51. Timpooneke Trail third waterfall

Directions: Follow the same directions as for No. 49.

Trail description: Continue up the trail from No. 50 for about 3 minutes to this waterfall pouring across the trail just before it switchbacks to the right, so that you have two different views of the falls, as you hike up the trail.

Distances: 39 mi. from SLC; 13 mi. from Alpine; 45 min. from trailhead.

Estimated height: 20 ft.

Map and trail guide: Timpanogos Cave (not shown); PAUT p.24, DAUT p.140–143, KLCL p.132–136.

Comments: See the comments for No. 49.

52. Timpooneke Trail fourth waterfall

p73L *Directions*: Follow the same directions as for No. 49.

Trail description: Continue up the trail from No. 51 for about 10 minutes to where the trail turns back to the east. The water fall is just past this switchback. Like No.

51, this falls crosses the trail twice, just before it switchbacks again.

Distances: 39 mi. from SLC; 13 mi. from Alpine; 55 min. from trailhead.

Estimated height: 50 ft.

Map and trail guide: Timpanogos Cave (not shown); PAUT p.24, DAUT p.140–143, KLCL p.132–136.

Comments: An especially beautiful waterfall, pouring over ledges of rocks at the top. See also the comments for No. 49.

53. Scout Falls

Directions: Follow the same directions as for No. 49.

Trail description: When the trail switchbacks at No. 52, go straight ahead where a very short spur trail leads to a view straight across at the falls.

Distances: 39 mi. from SLC; 13 mi. from Alpine; 55 min. from trailhead.

Estimated height: 100 ft.

Map and trail guide: Timpanogos Cave (shown); DAUT p.140–143, KLCL p.132–133.

Comments: A series of springs feed this waterfall in an alcove of the headwall of the valley. It is usually much diminished by mid summer. See also the comments for No. 49.

54. Aspen Grove Trail first waterfall

Directions: Follow the same directions as for No. 49, but instead of turning in at the Timpooneke trailhead, continue another 6 miles to the Aspen Grove trailhead, a good-sized parking lot between mileposts 22 and 23.

Trail description: From the center of the parking lot, hike west on the wide trail; in a few feet a sign indicates Stewart Cascades to the left, Aspen Grove trail straight ahead. Proceed straight ahead on the paved trail, which climbs steadily but steeply to the waterfall at the first switchback. In about 15 minutes you will see the waterfall ahead; in about 30 minutes you should reach it.

Distances: 45 mi. from SLC; 19 mi. from Alpine; 30 min. from trailhead.

Estimated height: 50–60 ft.

Map and trail guide: Aspen Grove (not shown); DAUT p.140–143, PAUT p.228–229, KLCL p.34–37.

Comments: A September weekday is the best time to view this waterfall; both the snow fields and the crowds have gone by then. If there is snow pack at the foot of the falls, be careful not to approach it; people have been killed falling through the snow to the rocks below. A recreation pass, or a federal pass, is required for access to this trailhead. This trail is also known as the Timpanogos Summit Trail.

55. Aspen Grove Trail second waterfall

p73R *Directions*: Follow the same directions as for No. 54.

Trail description: Follow the same directions as for No. 54. Continue another 10 minutes up the trail, as it switchbacks to the next level and the next waterfall.

Distances: 45 mi. from SLC; 19 mi. from Alpine; 40 min. from trailhead.

Estimated height: 40 ft.

Map and trail guide: Aspen Grove (not shown); DAUT p.140–143, PAUT p.28–29, KLCL p.12, 34–36.

Comments: See the comments for No. 54. These two waterfalls appear to be fed by springs, since there is no sign of a stream at the higher elevations. There are three other smaller waterfalls upstream from these two, but the trail does not go near them. They can be seen from a distance at the next switchback past this waterfall, and from a few places further up the trail. Earlier in the year there are many more waterfalls higher up the trail, but they are not perennial.

56. Aspen Grove Trail third waterfall

p74L *Directions*: Follow the same directions as for No. 54.

Trail description: Follow the same directions as for No. 55. Continue another 5–10 minutes up the trail, which in this section becomes rocky and washed-out. The waterfall comes down the side of the hill and crosses the trail.

Distances: 45 mi. from SLC; 19 mi. from Alpine; 50 min. from trailhead.

Estimated height: 25 ft.

Map and trail guide: Aspen Grove (not shown); DAUT p.140–143, PAUT p.28–29, KLCL p.34–36.

Comments: See the comments for No. 54. A fourth waterfall, upstream from this one, can be seen along the trail on the next level, after the next switchback. It is another 10–15 minutes further on.

1. Richards Hollow waterfall.

4. Adams Canyon lower waterfall.

6. Adams Canyon upper waterfall.

10. Church Fork upper waterfall.

13. Lake Blanche outlet waterfall.

14. Hidden Falls.

18. Doughnut Falls.

28. Peruvian Gulch waterfall.

29. Alta City waterfall.

32. Ely Creek waterfall.

36. Smooth Rock Falls.

41. Provo River Falls upper waterfall.

42. Provo River Falls middle waterfall.

43. Provo River Falls lower waterfall.

46. Battle Creek Canyon first waterfall.

47. Battle Creek Canyon second falls.

52. Timpooneke Trail fourth waterfall.

55. Aspen Grove Trail second waterfall.

56. Aspen Grove Trail third waterfall.

64. Bridal Veil Falls.

67. Fifth Water middle falls.

68. Fifth Water upper falls.

70. Chicken Creek waterfall.

74. Cascade Falls [Navajo Lake].

80. Lower Emerald Pool waterfall.

81. Upper Emerald Pool waterfall.

82. Menu Falls.

86. Sulphur Creek lower waterfall.

88. Singletree Falls.

92. Lower Calf Creek Falls.

97. Mill Creek first waterfall.

99. Kens Lake waterfall.

57. Stewart Falls

Directions: Follow the same directions as for No. 54.

Trail description: From the center of the parking lot, hike west on the wide trail; in a few feet a sign indicates Stewart Cascades to the left, Aspen Grove trail straight ahead. Turn left. The trail soon climbs and passes above the amphitheater, then contours around the mountain to the south. In about 45 minutes you have your first view of the falls. In another 5 minutes there is a closer view. In another 7 minutes you come to a high viewpoint beside the falls. A steep trail leads down for about 5 minutes to the foot of the falls, which is the best view.

Distances: 45 mi. from SLC; 19 mi. from Alpine; 70 min. from the trailhead.

Estimated height: 100 ft.

Map and trail guide: Aspen Grove (shown as Stewarts Cascades); KEBE p.57–60, PAUT p.30–32, KLCL p.54–56, 60–61.

Comments: All roads are paved to the trailhead. A recreation pass, or a federal park pass, is required to drive and park in this area.

58. Cascade Springs upper cascades

Directions: From exit 287 of I-15 drive east 18 miles on Highway 92 to the top of the pass on the Alpine Scenic Loop. Just over the pass turn left (east) onto Road 114 and drive for 7 miles to the parking area at Cascade Springs.

Trail description: Go downhill from the parking lot and follow the trails past the lower section of the springs. From the bridge there is a good view of the lower section of the cascades. Cross the bridge and go uphill along the stream and back downhill on the other side for more views of cascades in this steep section of the stream. Side trails in a few places lead down to the stream for closer views.

Distances: 48 mi. from SLC; 22 mi. from Alpine; 5–10 min. from trailhead.

Estimated height: 10 ft. cascade.

Map and trail guide: Aspen Grove (shown); BESC p.176–183, KEBE p.60–62, WHUT p.135., KLCL p.191–192.

Comments: All roads are paved to the trailhead. A recreation pass, or a federal pass, is required in this area.

59. Cascade Springs middle cascades

Directions: Follow the same directions as for No. 58.

Trail description: Go down the hill from the parking lot and follow the boardwalks through the lower part of the springs.

Distances: 48 mi. from SLC; 22 mi. from Alpine; 5 min. from trailhead.

Estimated height: 2 ft.

Map and trail guide: Aspen Grove (shown); BESC p.176–183, KEBE p.60–62, WHUT p.135, KLCL p.191–192.

Comments: See the comments for No. 58.

60. Cascade Springs outlet waterfall

Directions: Follow the same directions as for No. 58.

Trail description: Go down the hill from the parking lot and turn left through the grass instead of crossing the first bridge. There are two places where small falls pour over the edge of the limestone ledges at the lower end of the springs area.

Distances: 48 mi. from SLC; 22 mi. from Alpine; 3 min. from trailhead.

Estimated height: 5 ft.

Map and trail guide: Aspen Grove (shown); BESC p.176–183, KEBE p.60–62, WHUT p.135, KLCL p.191–192.

Comments: See the comments for No. 58.

61. Pine Hollow waterfall

Directions: From exit 287 of I-15 drive east on Highway 92 (the Alpine Scenic Loop) for 15 miles. Just past the parking lot for the Pine Hollow Trailhead, a thin waterfall cascades down Pine Hollow on the left side of the road, just before milepost 15. A pullout is beside the waterfall.

Trail description: Roadside.

Distances: 38 mi. from SLC; 12 mi. from Alpine; roadside.

Estimated height: 30 ft.

Map and trail guide: Timpanogos Cave (not shown); BESC p.176–182.

Comments: All roads are paved to the waterfall. A recreation pass, or a federal pass, is required in this area.

62. Alpine Scenic Loop first waterfall

Directions: Follow the same directions as for No. 61. Continue to the next side stream, just past milepost 15. There is a pullout with a tree beside the waterfall.

Trail description: Roadside.

Distances: 38 mi. from SLC; 12 mi. from Alpine; roadside.

Estimated height: 15 ft.

Map and trail guide: Timpanogos Cave (not shown); BESC p.176–182.

Comments: See the comments for No. 61.

63. Alpine Scenic Loop second waterfall

Directions: Follow the same directions as for No. 62. Continue to the next side stream, between mileposts 15 and 16. There is a pullout beside this small cascade.

Trail description: Roadside.

Distances: 38 mi. from SLC; 12 mi. from Alpine; roadside.

Estimated height: 3 ft.

Map and trail guide: Timpanogos Cave (not shown); BESC p.176–182.

Comments: See the comments for No. 61.

64. Bridal Veil Falls

p74R *Directions*: From exit 275 of I-15, drive east on Highway 52 about 4 miles to the junction with Highway 189. Continue east into Provo Canyon about 3 miles to a parking lot on the right for Nunns Park. Park on the south side of the highway, not the section of the park beyond the underpass.

Trail description: Above the parking lot is the paved Provo River Parkway Trail. Hike up canyon on this trail about 5 minutes to the foot of the falls.

Distances: 42 mi. from SLC; 5 mi. from Orem; 5 min. from trailhead (or roadside).

Estimated height: 600 ft., according to guidebooks.

Map and trail guide: Bridal Veil Falls (shown); BESC p.176–181, KLCL p.159–161.

Comments: All roads are paved to the trailhead. The falls can also be seen from a good viewpoint a little further up the highway.

65. Upper Falls

Directions: Follow the directions for No. 64. About half a mile past Bridal Veil Falls a parking area on the left (north) side of the highway provides a view of Upper Falls on the south side of the canyon. A left turn lane provides access to the parking lot.

Trail description: Roadside view.

Distances: 43 mi. from SLC; 6 mi. from Orem; roadside.

Estimated height: 40 ft.

Map and trail guide: Bridal Veil

Falls (shown); PAUT p.39.

Comments: All roads are paved to the trailhead. It might be possible to hike to the falls from the Provo River Parkway Trail but the trail described by the Paxmans and Taylors no longer exists.

Other waterfalls of the area. The Paxmans and Taylors mention a waterfall in Deer Creek (PAUT p.38); I hiked to it many years ago but was unable to locate it in 1998; perhaps the floods of 1983 destroyed it. Kelsey (KLCL) mentions cascades or waterfalls in Slide Canyon (p.67–68), Lost Creek (p.71–72), and Grove Creek (p.92–93). He also mentions a waterfall in the cirque above Stewart Falls (KLCL p.55–57); this can be seen in summer from the foot of the lift at Sundance.

Waterfalls of Central Utah

66. Fifth Water lower falls

Directions: From exit 261 of I-15 drive 11 miles east on Highway 6 to the marked turnoff to Diamond Fork (at about milepost 183). Drive north about 10 miles to the Three Forks parking lot.

Trail description: From the parking lot, cross a small bridge to the trail along the left (north) side of Sixth Water. (A second bridge leading to the right should be ignored.) In about 30 minutes cross Sixth Water on another bridge and continue along Fifth Water to a hot springs area, reached in about another 40 minutes. At the lower end of of the open area, turn aside to the stream for a view of this series of cascades.

Distances: 70 mi. from SLC; 22 mi. from Springville; 65 min. from the trailhead.

Estimated height: 15 ft. in several cascades.

Map and trail guide: Rays Valley (not shown); KEBE, p. 99–101.

Comments: All roads are paved to the trailhead. A beautiful trail, generally level and well shaded by deciduous trees. There are hot springs at the waterfall; the sulphur smell begins half a mile before the falls. In both

Sixth Water and Fifth Water there are numerous cascades and small falls that are worth viewing. Two of the most notable are just downstream from the hot springs falls. (But be cautious about leaving the trail for a closer look; steep banks and poison ivy are hazards.) This is a popular trail with a moderately small parking area; weekdays would be better for a visit.

67. Fifth Water middle falls

p75L *Directions*: Follow the same directions as for No. 66.

Trail description: Follow the directions for No. 66. After turning aside to No. 66, continue on up the trail to the larger waterfall, easily in sight by now.

Distances: 70 mi. from SLC; 22 mi. from Springville; 70 min. from the trailhead.

Estimated height: 15 ft.

Map and trail guide: Rays Valley (shown); KEBE p. 99–101, WHUT p.132.

Comments: See the comments for No. 67.

68. Fifth Water upper falls

p75R *Directions*: Follow the same directions as for No. 66.

Trail description: Follow the same directions as for No. 67. From the hot springs continue up the trail on the left for another 5 minutes to a view of the falls from the trail.

Distances: 70 mi. from SLC; 22 mi. from Springville; 75 min. from the trailhead.

Estimated height: 50 ft.

Map and trail guide: Rays Valley (shown); mentioned briefly with a photograph but no directions in BRMO p.77–81.

Comments: A beautiful two-tiered waterfall, set among green trees, with an excellent viewing point from the trail. See the comments for No. 67.

69. Ford Creek waterfall

Directions: From exit 261 of I-15, drive southeast on Highway 6 for 50 miles, into Price Canyon. Between mileposts 223 and 224 the highway passes around a curve through a road-

cut. The waterfall is in the middle of the roadcut. Although it can be seen while driving by, it is safer to stop in a pullout on either side of the roadcut and walk to the waterfall.

Trail description: Roadside.

Distances: 99 mi. from SLC; 6 mi. from Price; roadside.

Estimated height: 30 ft.

Map and trail guide: Kyune (not shown).

Comments: In the winter this is a popular falls for ice climbing.

70. Chicken Creek waterfall

76L *Directions*: From exit 222 of I-15 drive south 9 miles (on the east side of the freeway) on Highway 28 to the center of Levan. Drive east on 100 South for 4 miles into Chicken Creek to a view of the waterfall on the south side of the road. (One mile out of town turn right into Chicken Creek rather than Pigeon Creek.)

Trail description: The waterfall is visible from the road. There are various parking places near the top and foot of the falls, from which you can hike to the falls within 5 minutes.

Distances: 101 mi. from SLC; 4 mi. from Levan; roadside.

Estimated height: 20 ft.

Map and trail guide: Levan (not shown); mentioned briefly in HUUT p.64–65.

Comments: The last 3 miles are unpaved. I suspect this is not a natural waterfall. It looks as though an earthen dam was built across the original course of the creek; the water behind the dam then created a spillway over the rocks beside the original channel. You can also reach Levan from exit 207, if approaching from the south.

71. Milky Falls

Directions: From exit 225 of I-15 drive southeast for 29 miles on Highway 132 through Moroni to Highway 89. Drive south on 89 for 12 miles to Manti. Drive east on 5th South into Manti Canyon. At 6 miles, pass Manti Community Campground (N.F.). Within the next mile, the road divides; continue on the right hand (south) fork. You will come to a parking area with a sign that says "Milky Falls/Trail No. 131." This is *not* the trail to the falls; continue driving another mile to the top of several switchbacks (about 8 miles from Manti) where there is an open space with a view of the falls, a parking area, and a large sign that says "Milky Falls/150 yards." Park here.

Trail description: Follow the trail downhill for about 3 minutes to the base of the falls.

Distances: 134 mi. from SLC; 8 mi. from Manti; 3 min. from trailhead.

Estimated height: 100 ft.

Map and trail guide: Black Mountain (shown); information from GNIS.

Comments: The last 7 miles to the trailhead are unpaved; there are a few rough spots, but the road generally is a well graded gravel road. Although the upper part of the falls can be seen from the road, be sure to walk the short distance for a complete view.

72. Bullion Falls

Directions: From exit 23 of I-70 drive south for 12 miles on Highway 89 to the center of Marysvale. Drive west on Center Street and follow the signs for 6 miles to where the road crosses a bridge ¼ mile before the Miners' Park picnic area. There is a parking area just across the bridge.

Trail description: Go back across the bridge and hike uphill on an old jeep road past a mine dump and other mine buildings. The road eventually deteriorates to a trail. After about 30 minutes you will come to a viewpoint from which you have a good view of the falls. An undeveloped trail leads steeply downhill to a closer view.

Distances: 219 mi. from SLC; 6 mi. from Marysvale; 30 min. from the trailhead.

Estimated height: 40 ft.

Map and trail guide: Mount Brigham (shown); BIFI p. 91–92, HUUT p.110–111.

Comments: The last 5 miles are unpaved, and may be littered with fallen rocks and branches. Four miles out of Marysvale, at the National Forest boundary, is a display with tour guides; be sure to pick one up for useful information about the area.

73. Cascade Falls [Marysvale]

Directions: Follow the same directions as for No. 72.

Trail description: About halfway to Bullion Falls, just past the top of the switchback past the mine dump, Cascade Falls can be seen halfway up the opposite canyon wall.

Distances: 219 mi. from SLC; 6 mi. from Marysvale; 15 min. from the trailhead.

Estimated height: 10 ft.

Map and trail guide: Mount Brigham (not shown); information from tour guide.

Comments: It might be possible to get to a closer view of the falls by hiking upstream from Miner's Park. See the comments for No. 73.

Other waterfalls of the area. Biddle (BIFI p.112–113) describes a hike to a view of a waterfall in Fall Canyon out of Fillmore; in early September we found the trail he describes long abandoned and overgrown, and no flow of water in Fall Canyon. The GNIS lists two waterfalls on the Bull Rush Peak topo: Marys Veil and Pillings Cascade, but with no latitude or longitude; they are not shown on the topo, and enquiries at the National Forest ranger station in Panguitch yielded no one who knew anything about them. Cunningham/Burke and Tilton mention waterfalls in Water Canyon (CUWI p.262–264, TIUT p.228), a tributary of the Price River, and in South Cedar Ridge Canyon (CUWI p.332–334, TIUT p.156–157). Tilton also mentions waterfalls on the Left Fork of Huntington National Recreation Trail (TIUT p.144–145) and in Mill Fork Canyon (TIUT p.148).

Waterfalls of Southwest Utah

74. Cascade Falls [Navajo Lake]

p76R *Directions*: From exit 59 of I-15 drive east about 1 mile to Center Street in Cedar City. Turn south two blocks to Highway 14. Drive east 27 miles to the Duck Creek Campground and Visitor Center (between mileposts 27 and 28). Turn right (south) beside the visitor center and drive 2 miles to Road 054; turn left and drive another mile to the large parking lot at the edge of the plateau.

Trail description: From the parking lot follow the trail west for 10 minutes. As it rounds a corner you have a first view of the falls in the distance. In another 5 or 10 minutes you should reach a viewing platform at the point where the falls pours out of an underground river halfway down the cliff.

Distances: 282 mi. from SLC; 30 mi. from Cedar City; 20 min. from trailhead.

Estimated height: 50 ft.

Map and trail guide: Navajo Lake (shown); BESC p.32–39, MANF p.122, KEBE p.150–153.

Comments: The last 3 miles to the trailhead are unpaved. This area is closed by snow much of the year. The falls are presumed to be an outlet from Navajo Lake.

75. The Falls

Directions: From exit 59 of I-15 drive east about 1 mile to Center Street in Cedar City. Drive south two blocks to Highway 14. Drive east 41 miles to Highway 89, then south 14 miles to the north end of Glendale. Between mileposts 90 and 91, turn east on 300 North (aka Bench Road, Route 1870). Drive east 8 miles on a good graded road to where the road descends a hill into a broad valley. When the road crosses Kanab Creek in the center of the valley, find a place to park. A side road just south of the main road is a possible place.

Trail description: Walk downstream a few feet to where the stream suddenly drops over a cliff. The best viewpoint is on the west side of the stream, where a fence comes up to the edge of the cliff.

Distances: 315 mi. from SLC; 8 mi. from Glendale; 1 min. from parking area.

Estimated height: 40 ft.

Map and trail guide: Bald Knoll (shown); information from the GNIS.

Comments: One of the few officially named waterfalls in Utah, appearing both in the GNIS and on the topo map as "The Falls." One of the strangest falls in Utah, appearing suddenly in the middle of a sagebrush cow pasture.

76. Quail Creek first waterfall

Directions: From exit 23 of I-15, drive south through Leeds for 2 miles on old Highway 91 along the east side of the freeway. Turn west at the sign to Red Cliffs Campground, drive through a narrow underpass beneath the freeway and continue for 2 miles to the campground. Park in the lot designated for hikers.

Trail description: Follow the constructed trail upstream for 10 minutes to the waterfall.

Distances: 291 mi. from SLC; 4 mi. from Leeds; 10 min. from trailhead.

Estimated height: 7 ft.

Map and trail guide: Harrisburg Junction (not shown); CUWI p.83–85.

Comments: All roads are paved to the trailhead. Cunningham and Burke list this as a spring waterfall, but I found it still flowing in the fall.

77. Quail Creek second waterfall

Directions: Follow the same directions as for No. 76.

Trail description: Follow the same directions as for No. 76. Continue upstream for another 10 minutes to the second waterfall. The trail is less clear here. Stay close to the stream, walking in it if necessary, for the most direct route.

Distances: 291 mi. from SLC; 4 mi. from Leeds; 20 min. from trailhead.

Estimated height: 8 ft.

Map and trail guide: Harrisburg Junction (not shown); CUWI p.83–85.

Comments: See the comment for No. 76.

Other waterfalls in the area. Several authors mention Kitchen Falls (KLHP p.70–71, URTR p.142–144, TIUT p.202–203). Kelsey (KLHP) also mentions waterfalls in Snake Creek Canyon (p.50, 55), Hogeye Canyon (p.94–95), and Starlight Canyon (p.78–79, 224). Benson (BESC p.32–37) mentions spring waterfalls in Cedar Canyon; they're between mileposts 7 and 10 when driving out of Cedar City. Hall (HAHI p.174–177) and Molvar/Martin (MOHI p.158–163, 169–170) mention waterfalls in the Ashdown Gorge Wilderness. Cunningham and Burke (CUWI p.100–101) mention waterfalls in Water Canyon on Canaan Mtn. Urmann mentions waterfalls in Deer Creek Canyon, a tributary of the Paria (p.141–142).

Waterfalls of Zion National Park

78. Camp Creek waterfall

Directions: From exit 42 of I-15 drive north for 2 miles on the frontage road (old Highway 91) east of the freeway (toward Kanarraville). Turn east on 1925 South (aka Wipishani Lane) and drive 1 mile to the trailhead, a circular parking area around a tree, where the dirt road turns left.

Trail description: Walk south through a gate beside the parking area, and follow a trail around the corner into the mouth of Camp Creek Canyon. The waterfall is about a 4 minute walk from the trailhead. There is one small stream crossing, so you may have to jump rocks or get your feet wet.

Distances: 271 mi. from SLC; 21 mi. from Cedar City; 5 min. from trailhead.

Estimated height: 30 ft.

Map and trail guide: Kanarraville (not shown); MOHI p.145–147.

Comments: The last few hundred feet to the trailhead are unpaved. Molvar and Martin actually describe the trail in Camp Creek above the falls. Their description is useful only for locating the trailhead and the existence of the falls.

79. Taylor Creek Middle Fork waterfall

Directions: From exit 40 of I-15, drive east 2 miles to the Taylor Creek trailhead, well marked on the left.

Trail description: Follow the trail downhill and upstream along Taylor Creek for about 40 minutes to the Larson cabin at the junction of the North Fork and the Middle Fork. Continue on the trail for about 15 more minutes. Watch for shelving rock on the left. Go off the trails a short way to see the falls.

Distances: 272 mi. from SLC; 22 mi. from Cedar City; 55 min. from trailhead.

Estimated height: 5–10 ft.

Map and trail guide: Kolob Arch (not shown); KEBE p.135–137, BRUT p.110 (briefly), MOHI p.135–138.

Comments: All roads are paved to the trailhead. Entrance fee required. There are numerous stream crossings; plan on wading boots in the spring. Later in the year you should be able to cross on stepping stones.

80. Lower Emerald Pool waterfall

p77L *Directions*: From exit 27 of I-15 drive southeast 6 miles to La Verkin and the junction with Highway 9. Continue east on Highway 9 for 20 miles to the Zion National Park entrance station. One mile past the entrance station turn north into Zion Canyon and continue 3 miles to the Emerald Pools trailhead. Parking is available on both sides of the road.

Trail description: Follow the signs for a 15–20 minute walk on a paved trail to the waterfall. Continue on the trail behind the falls and cross to the opposite side for good views.

Distances: 313 mi. from SLC; 6 mi. from Springdale; 20 min. from trailhead.

Estimated height: 20 ft.

Map and trail guide: Temple of Sinawava (not shown); ADUT p.44–46, LIHI p.14–15, KEBE p.138–141, WHUT p.36, 39, MOHI p.51–55.

Comments: All roads are paved to the trailhead and the trail itself is paved to the Lower Emerald Pool. The flow of water is much reduced in the summer and fall. Entrance fee required.

81. Upper Emerald Pool waterfall

p77R *Directions*: Follow the directions for No. 80.

Trail description: From the far side of No. 80 continue on a steep trail uphill for another 20–25 minutes to the Upper Pool, where a waterfall drops out of a cleft in the cliffs.

Distances: 313 mi. from SLC; 6 mi. from Springdale; 40 min. from trailhead.

Estimated height: 100 ft.

Map and trail guide: Temple of Sinawava (not shown); ADUT p.44–46, LIHI p.14–15, KEBE p.138–141, WHUT p.36,38, MOHI p.51–55.

Comments: See the comments for No. 80.

82. Menu Falls

p78L *Directions*: Follow the directions for No. 80. Continue another 3 miles past the Emerald Pools parking areas to a long narrow parking area on the left, about halfway between Weeping Rock and the Temple of Sinawava. It is easier to access the parking area when returning from the Temple of Sinawava. There is no sign at the parking area or the trailhead.

Trail description: Climb a short trail to wooden viewing platforms in front of the two waterfalls.

Distances: 316 mi. from SLC; 9 mi. from Springdale; 2 min. from the trailhead.

Estimated height: 10–15 ft.

Map and trail guide: Temple of Sinawava (not shown); found by serendipity — photos appear in several photography books.

Comments: This is a fragile area; please stay on the viewing platforms. I've been told the name results from the falls having once appeared as a standard photo on the cover of the Zion Lodge restaurant menu. All roads are paved to the trailhead. Entrance fee required.

83. Temple of Sinawava spring waterfall

Directions: Follow the directions for No. 82. Continue another mile to the end of the road at the Temple of Sinawava parking lot.

Trail description: Roadside. The waterfall can be seen for a couple of months in the spring straight ahead at the end of the parking lot.

Distances: 317 mi. from SLC; 10 mi. from Springdale; roadside.

Estimated height: 100+ ft.

Map and trail guide: Temple of Sinawava (not shown).

Comments: Although this is not a perennial waterfall, it is so frequently photographed, so spectacular, and so easy to view, that I have included it. All roads are paved to the waterfall. Entrance fee required.

Spring waterfalls in Zion National Park. Early in the year, in April, spring runoff creates temporary waterfalls in the canyon. Most noticeable are the following. At the view area for Court of the Patriarchs, two falls can be seen in the distance between the Patriarchs and Temple of the Virgin. In the canyon containing Emerald Pools a fall can be seen on the right side of the canyon; the falls at the Lower and Upper Pools, which become a mist later in the year, are strong at this time. There is a waterfall over the top of Weeping Rock.

Other waterfalls in Zion National Park. See Adkison (ADUT), Molvar/Martin (MOHI), Brereton (BREX) and Kelsey (KLCA) for details of hiking to the following: Zion Narrows (Big Spring, unnamed waterfall, falls at the mouths of Orderville Canyon and Mystery Canyon); Left Fork North Creek (aka Great West Canyon) (Archangel Cascades, Keyhole Falls); Right Fork North Creek (Double Falls and Barrier Falls); waterfalls in Coalpits Wash; Labyrinth Falls in Parunuweap Canyon; Deep Creek; La Verkin Creek. Day (DAUT p.327–332) also describes the Zion Narrows hike. Some of these may be reachable by day hiking; others are only for groups with rappelling experience. Beartrap Falls in the Kolob section can be approached from several different routes, but seems too far for day hiking from any direction.

Waterfalls of South Central Utah

These waterfalls can all be accessed from Torrey. Directions are given from there; if coming from Escalante, recalculate mileages from milepost 60 of Highway 12.

Recommended route to Torrey: From Salt Lake City drive south 122 miles on I-15 to Scipio (exit 188), then southeast 28 miles on Highway 50 (mileposts 31 to 59) to Salina. From the west side of Salina drive southeast 69 miles on Highway 24 to Torrey (milepost 69). Total mileage from Salt Lake City is 219 miles.

84. Sulphur Creek upper waterfall

Directions: From Torrey, drive 9 miles east on Highway 24 to the Chimney Rock parking lot on the left (north) between mileposts 77 and 78. Park here.

Trail description: Cross the highway and hike downhill for 40 minutes in the dry wash leading to Sulphur Creek. Hike downstream in Sulphur Creek for 80 minutes to the waterfall. From here you can either return to your car, or bypass the falls on the right and continue downstream to the other two waterfalls and the Capitol Reef Visitor Center.

Distances: 228 mi. from SLC; 9 mi. from Torrey; 2 hours from trailhead.

Estimated height: 10 ft.

Map and trail guide: Twin Rocks (not shown); ADUT p.130–131, KLCA p.50–51.

Comments: All roads are paved to the trailhead. My experience was that the hike downstream to all three waterfalls was more difficult than expected, on the basis of descriptions in the guidebooks.

85. Sulphur Creek middle waterfall

Directions: Follow the same directions as for No. 84.

Trail description: Follow the same directions as for No. 84. Continue downstream another 15 minutes to the second waterfall. At this point you are in the narrows and mostly walking in the creek. From here you can either return to your car, or bypass the falls on the right and continue downstream to the third waterfall and the Capitol Reef Visitor Center.

Distances: 228 mi. from SLC; 9 mi. from Torrey; 2 hours 15 min. from trailhead.

Estimated height: 10 ft.

Map and trail guide: Twin Rocks (not shown); ADUT p.130–131, KLCA p.50–51.

Comments: If you continue downstream from this waterfall you will be walking in the creek much of the way. There are several other notable small waterfalls and cascades between here and the lower waterfall. It's another hour and 45 minutes downstream to the lower waterfall.

86. Sulphur Creek lower waterfall

p78R *Directions*: From Torrey drive 11 miles east on Highway 24 to the entrance to Capitol Reef National Park (near milepost 80). Park across the highway from the Visitor Center, where the highway bridge crosses Sulphur Creek.

Trail description: Cross under the bridge and hike upstream for about 30 minutes to the first waterfall. There are a number of stream crossings. The stream is fairly shallow, so it may be possible to cross on stepping stones, but wading boots are recommended.

Distances: 230 mi. from SLC; 11 mi. from Torrey; 30 min. from the trailhead.

Estimated height: 6 ft.

Map and trail guide: Twin Rocks (not shown); ADUT p.130–131, KLCA p.50–51.

Comments: There are two other waterfalls (Nos. 84 and 85) upstream. If you want to continue to them you can bypass this waterfall by climbing up the rock ledges on either side or (more safely) by backtracking to where the slopes on the south side of the creek come down to the water's edge and following a faint trail along them to the top of the waterfall. From here to the next waterfall is a hike of another hour and 45 minutes, much of it in the creek. It is more customary to hike downstream to all three waterfalls from the Chimney Rock parking lot, using a car shuttle to get back from the Visitor Center.

87. Fremont River waterfall

Directions: From Torrey drive 18 miles east on Highway 24 to a large parking area on the left side of a curve between mileposts 86 and 87.

Trail description: The waterfall can be seen from the far corner of the parking area. A trail leads down a sandhill and through some willows to a pebbled beach at the foot of the falls.

Distances: 237 mi. from SLC; 18 mi. from Torrey; roadside, or 3 min. from trailhead.

Estimated height: 20 ft.

Map and trail guide: Fruita (shown); mentioned briefly in ADUT p.123.

Comments: I've been told that this is not part of the normal river channel, but a falls created by the redirection of the river when the highway was built. Nevertheless, it's well worth stopping to see.

88. Singletree Falls

p79L *Directions*: From Torrey drive east 1 mile to Highway 12, then south 12 miles to Singletree Campground at milepost 112. Park near the trailhead register across from the campground host.

Trail description: Follow the trail along the edge of the campground, climb a stile, and head downhill. After about 10 minutes, cross an old road and a side stream and continue downhill. In another 10 minutes switchback around to the right to the foot of the falls.

Distances: 232 mi. from SLC; 13 mi. from Torrey; 20 min. from the trailhead.

Estimated height: 30 ft.

Map and trail guide: Grover (not shown); MANA p.101.

Comments: All roads are paved to the trailhead. To shorten the walk, start from campsite #12 near the stile. There are lots of small loose rocks on this trail which require extra caution in the steeper sections.

89. Blue Spring Creek waterfall

Directions: From Torrey, drive east one mile to Highway 12, then south 40 miles over Boulder Mountain and past Boulder, to the Hell's Backbone Road (at milepost 84). Drive west 21 miles to a narrow pullout on the left side of the road, where there is a sign: Upper Box — Death Hollow Access.

Trail description: Hike for about 5–10 minutes downhill and downstream along Pine Creek to the trail register at the bottom of the hill. Then follow the trail down Pine Creek for another 10–15 minutes, crossing the creek about three times. Watch for where Blue Spring Creek comes in from the southwest. Cross Pine Creek again and walk a few yards up Blue Spring Creek to the foot of the falls.

Distances: 281 mi. from SLC; 62 mi. from Torrey (21 mi. from Escalante); 20 min. from the trailhead.

Estimated height: 20–25 ft.

Map and trail guide: Posy Lake (not shown); LAHI p.47, ADHI p.251–255.

Comments: The 21 miles on the Hell's Backbone Road are unpaved, and can be scary if you're not used to driving back roads in the mountains; but it's a good quality gravel road, easily driven by passenger cars. Pine Creek is deep and cold and full of rocks; wading boots will be necessary.

90. Pine Creek waterfall

Directions: Follow the same directions as for No. 89.

Trail description: From the parking area, hike downhill for about 3 minutes, watching for the waterfall on the left before the bottom of the hill.

Distances: 281 mi. from SLC; 62 mi. from Torrey (21 mi. from Escalante); 3 min. from the trailhead.

Estimated height: 5 ft.

Map and trail guide: Posy Lake (not shown); found by serendipity.

Comments: See the comments in No. 89 about the Hell's Backbone Road. There are no stream crossings to get to this waterfall.

91. Upper Calf Creek Falls

Directions: From Torrey, drive east one mile to Highway 12, then south 42 miles to where a faint road leads off the highway (between mileposts 81 and 82) to the canyon rim. You may want to park your passenger car just off the highway and walk the few hundred feet over the rough road to the rim and the trailhead register.

Trail description: From the trailhead register you can see a faint trail through the boulders leading down the slick rock slope and beyond it a further trail leading on toward the green oasis of Calf Creek. Follow the trail downhill for 10 minutes, then across country at a fairly level rate for another 20 minutes, then downhill for another 5 minutes to the foot of the falls. Just before you reach the lower rim of Calf Creek, the trail divides. Take the left-hand trail to reach the foot of the falls. If you find yourself in the open slick rock at the top of the falls, you've missed the junction and need to backtrack. When you reach the lower rim there is a tricky (but not especially dangerous) descent over a rock; at this point you should be able to see the falls ahead of you above the trees.

Distances: 262 mi. from SLC; 43 mi. from Torrey (6 mi. from Boulder); 35 min. from trail register.

Estimated height: 60 ft.

Map and trail guide: Calf Creek (shown); LAHI p.85–86, ADHI p.190–193, DAUT p.290, KLCA p.142–143, URTR p.36–39.

Comments: All roads are paved to the trailhead. Watch for poison ivy at the foot of the falls. Some authors describe this trail as "difficult" or "strenuous" but I agree with Adkison that it is moderately easy.

92. Lower Calf Creek Falls

p79R *Directions*: From Torrey, drive east one mile to Highway 12, then south 48 miles to the entrance to the Calf Creek campground (between milepost 75 and 76). Park in the lot at the entrance to the campground.

Trail description: This is a heavily traveled, straightforward trail. Walk toward the campground and watch for the trailhead register on the left. Take a trail guide; there are numbered interpretive signs every few minutes, and you'll want the trail guide to make use of them. It will take about 80 minutes of steady hiking to reach the falls, longer if you stop at the interpretive stops.

Distances: 268 mi. from SLC; 49 mi. from Torrey (12 mi. from Boulder); 80 min. from trailhead.

Estimated height: 126 ft., according to most guidebooks.

Map and trail guide: Calf Creek (shown); ADHI p.193–197, BESC p.51–52, BRUT p.122–123, DAUT p.288–290, KEBE p.165–167, LAHI p.80–81, WHUT p.142, KLCA p.142–143, URTR p.40–42.

Comments: All roads are paved to the trailhead. One of the most beautiful and most photographed waterfalls in Utah. A recreation pass is required.

93. Water Canyon [Bryce Canyon] waterfall

Directions: From exit 95 of I-15 drive east for 21 miles on Highway 20, south 17 miles on Highway 89, and east 18 miles on Highway 12 to the parking area on the right between mileposts 17 and 18.

Trail description: The trail is well developed. After it climbs uphill after the second stream crossing, take the right-hand fork for a view of the waterfall.

Distances: 271 mi. from SLC; 4 mi. from Tropic; 10 min. from trailhead.

Estimated height: 10–15 ft.

Map and trail guide: Tropic Canyon (not shown); ADUT, p.108–109.

Comments: All roads are paved to the trailhead. The bridges for the two stream crossings are presently (1998) destroyed by flash floods. There are logs across the stream, but they are not for the casual hiker. This waterfall is not a natural one; the stream is in a dry wash, the result of an irrigation diversion from the Sevier River.

Other waterfalls of the area. Both Kelsey (KLHU p.52–53) and Adkison (ADHI p.122–124) describe a waterfall in Hog Canyon; it was not flowing in June — perhaps the spring has dried up. There are small cascades in Willow Gulch on the way to Broken Bow Arch; Adkison (ADHI p.229–233) has the best trail description but doesn't mention the cascades; Lambrechte (LAHI p.159) also mentions them. Cunningham and Burke mention waterfalls in Fourmile Canyon (CUWI p.155–157) and in Beaver Wash Canyon (CUWI p.197–199). Day, Lambrechte, Adkison, and Urmann mention waterfalls in Death Hollow (DAUT p.291–295, LAHI p.51, 66, ADHI p.185–189, URTR p.47–50). Much-photographed waterfalls in Coyote Gulch (DAUT p.297–300, LAHI p.144, 147–148, KLCA p.160–161) may be accessible by day hiking from the trailhead to Stevens Arch on Fortymile Ridge; Adkison (ADHI p.211–221, 226–228) has a detailed trail description that mentions four separate waterfalls. Hall mentions waterfalls at the head of Pleasant Creek (HAHI p.140–142) and on Fish Creek (HAHI p.143–144), both of these on Boulder Mountain; they are reported to be only seasonal. Lambrechte, Adkison, and Urmann mention a small waterfall in Upper Gulch (LAHI p.91, ADHI p.174–179, URTR p.58–60). Lambrechte (LAHI) mentions cascades or waterfalls in Deep Creek (p.15, 48), Sand Creek (p.53), Fortymile Gulch (p.157; cf. also KLCA p.162–163) and West Boulder Creek (p.180). Kelsey mentions waterfalls in No Man's Canyon (KLHU p.32–34), Woodruff Canyon (KLHU p.35, 56–57), and Lower Gulch (KLCA p.144–145; although Urmann (p.61–63) implies this is a dryfall).

94. Professor Creek waterfall

Directions: From exit 180 of I-70, drive south 29 miles to Highway 128 (between mileposts 128 and 129). Drive north 18 miles along the east side of the Colorado River. Between mileposts 18 and 19 (past the turnoff to Castle Valley), turn right onto an unmarked dirt road. Drive up this road 2 miles, past the turnoff to Professor Valley Ranch, and park in a grove of cottonwoods just past the Canyonlands Field Institute yurts (tents).

Trail description: Follow the road a short way to the diversion facility. Then drop down to Professor Creek and follow it upstream for about 4.5 miles to where the waterfall drops around both sides of a large chock stone that blocks further travel upstream. The first half of the hike has well-worn trails along the banks. The second half goes through a section of narrows.

Distances: 248 mi. from SLC; 23 mi. from Moab; 2 hours, 15 min. from trailhead.

Estimated height: 10–15 ft.

Map and trail guide: Fisher Towers (not shown); KLCA p.62–63.

Comments: The last 2 miles to the trailhead are good quality dirt road. There are numerous stream crossings; wading boots are recommended. Avoid this hike if there is any chance of rain. About a mile before the waterfall is another smaller falls. This is a beautiful canyon hike.

95. Brumley Creek Arch waterfall

Directions: From exit 180 of I-70, drive south 39 miles on Highway 191, through Moab to the turnoff to the La Sal Mtn. Loop Road (County Road 126) at milepost 118. Turn left (east) for half a mile, then right. Continue up the Loop Road for 11 miles to where County Road 126 turns off it to the right as an unpaved road (signed to Geyser Pass). Turn right toward Geyser Pass and continue 1.3 miles to a bend in the road. Park here wherever you can get off the road.

Trail description: There is no trail, simply a bushwhacking route downhill through the scrub oak to the creek, the arch, and the waterfall. Begin by aiming uphill (southeast) to a group of aspen trees. From there hike downhill (south) to the rim of the canyon. Look upstream for a rock outcropping which you will pass on the uphill side. From there work your way gradually downhill and upstream (east) until you find a way down to the level of the stream. Continue upstream to Brumley Arch, high on the left wall. If you angle correctly, it will take about 40–45 minutes to reach the creek and another 5 minutes to get upstream to the arch. The waterfall is behind the right-hand buttress of the arch. It is almost impossible to reach, since access is blocked by large fallen trees in the creek and by rocks in the creek bottom too slippery to stand on. It can be viewed by climbing up the very steep opposite bank.

Distances: 251 mi. from SLC; 21 mi. from Moab; 50 min. from trailhead.

Estimated height: 40 ft.

Map and trail guide: Mount Tukuhnikivatz (not shown); word of mouth.

Comments: The last 1.3 miles to the trailhead are unpaved. This is a difficult bushwhacking route; better not go alone. Expect to get very wet if you try to get to the foot of the waterfall. Expect to wade the creek to get any sort of view of the waterfall.

96. Oowah Lake Road waterfall

Directions: From exit 180 of I-70, drive south 39 miles on Highway 191, through Moab to the turnoff to the La Sal Mtn. Loop Road (County Road 126) at milepost 118. Turn left (east) for half a mile, then right. Continue up the Loop

Road for 12 miles to the road that turns off to Oowah Lake. Park in the little pulloff just at the junction.

Trail description: Look down into the stream coming down from Oowah Lake for a view of this double falls.

Distances: 251 mi. from SLC; 21 mi. from Moab; roadside.

Estimated height: 15 ft.

Map and trail guide: Mount Tukuhnikivatz (not shown); found by serendipity.

Comments: A small section of road just before the turnoff is unpaved. There is no trail to the foot of the falls; the canyon here is a steep-walled narrows.

97. Mill Creek first waterfall

p80L *Directions*: From exit 180 of I-70, drive south 31 miles to the center of Moab near milepost 126. Turn east on Center Street to 400 East, then south to 400 South, then east on 400 South, which becomes Millcreek Dr. Turn right at the stop sign in order to stay on Millcreek Dr. Watch for a water tank high on the left. Just before reaching it, turn left onto Powerhouse Lane. Continue on Powerhouse Lane to the large parking area. It's about 3 miles from the center of town to the parking area.

Trail description: Hike east (upstream) from the parking area for about 10 minutes, past a building painted with folk art and a dam spillway, to where the trail crosses a bench away from the stream. Continue across the bench for about 5 minutes until the trail comes back down beside the stream. In a few minutes it comes down to the stream at a broad and shallow area. This is the best place to cross, although you may get your feet wet doing so. Continue through the grove of trees on the other side of the stream and follow the well-worn trail across a low bench on the other side. When the trail comes back down to stream level, continue beside the stream to the foot of the falls. For another view of the falls, backtrack for a few minutes, watching for a bypass trail that climbs the rock above the stream. From here you can climb to a good viewpoint of the falls.

Distances: 233 mi. from SLC; 3 mi. from Moab; 25 min. from trailhead.

Estimated height: 15 ft.

Map and trail guide: Rill Creek (not shown); KEBE p.210–212, KLCA p.64–65.

Comments: The last half mile or so to the trailhead is unpaved. There is poison ivy in places along this trail.

98. Mill Creek second waterfall

Directions: Follow the same directions as for No. 97.

Trail description: From the foot of No. 97, backtrack to the bypass trail and continue up the canyon for about 15 minutes. Watch for two large alcoves in the right hand wall of the canyon. About halfway between them the main trail descends a steep sandhill to cross a side drainage. After ascending out of the drainage, watch for a faint footpath on the left, leading off the trail to the foot of a large sloping slick rock area. Climb up this slick rock area and continue up canyon to where it seems to end at the corner of the cliffs. There is a trail here that leads around the corner to bypass a narrows section where the second waterfall is located. In a few minutes you should see the waterfall below you with a trail leading back to it from the bypass trail. Continue down these trails to the top of the falls. Here you can cross the stream and climb down some small ledges to the foot of the falls. It's an additional 15 minutes from the beginning of the bypass to the falls.

Distances: 233 mi. from SLC; 3 mi. from Moab; 55 min. from trailhead.

Estimated height: 7 ft.

Map and trail guide: Rill Creek (not shown); word of mouth.

Comments: See the comments for No. 97.

99. Kens Lake waterfall

p80R *Directions*: From exit 180 of I-70, drive south 39 miles on Highway 191, through Moab to the turnoff to the La Sal Mtn. Loop Road (County Road 126) at milepost 118. Turn left (east) for half a mile, then right. About two miles from Highway 191, turn left onto (unsigned) County Road 175. Go straight up this road for a little over a mile. By now the waterfall should be in sight ahead. A side road with a pullout is a possible place to park.

Trail description: There is no official trail to the waterfall. You can walk to it cross country in about 10 minutes. There are several intersecting dirt roads that could be walked to the waterfall but the easiest is to just follow sight lines.

Distances: 241 mi. from SLC; 11 mi. from Moab; 10 min. from County Road 175.

Estimated height: 35 ft.

Map and trail guide: Kane Springs (not shown); word of mouth.

Comments: The last mile is unpaved. This attractive waterfall is not natural, but is formed from a diversion tunnel channeling water from upper Mill Creek to Kens Lake and therefore is not always running.

100. Owl Creek waterfall

Directions: From exit 180 of I-70, drive south 110 miles, through Moab, Monticello and Blanding, to Highway 95 (between mileposts 47 and 48). Drive northwest 28 miles on Highway 95 to Highway 261 between mileposts 93 and 94. Drive south on 261 for 5 miles to the (unmarked) turnoff to Owl Creek trailhead. The turnoff is between mileposts 27 and 28, a mile past the Kane Gulch Ranger Station. Drive east on this dirt road for 5 miles to the trailhead parking area.

Trail description: This is the most remote and difficult-to-reach waterfall in the book. It's definitely not a hike to do alone, nor in the heat of summer, and not a hike to do unless you're an experienced hiker in the canyonlands area of Utah. The waterfall itself had a very small flow of water when we were there in October, so it's probably not worth visiting just for its own sake. From the center of the parking lot, walk east and then turn downhill (right) in the first drainage. Hike for about 5–10 minutes to the head of the canyon to which the drainage leads. Turn left and look for the cairned route down into the canyon. Climb down this route for about 35 minutes to the bottom of the canyon, passing a kiva with rock art about a third of the way down. Continue down this canyon for about 15 minutes to the main canyon of Owl Creek. Continue down Owl Creek for another 70 minutes to where it drops over a high dryfall. This is the first falls shown on the topo, and apparently flows in the spring. Turn left into a side canyon to bypass this dryfall. It will take about 30 minutes to reach the foot of the dryfall and another 15 to reach the second waterfall. Plan on a total of 3 hours to reach it from the trailhead, and 4 hours to get back up out of the canyons.

Distances: 347 mi. from SLC; 42 mi. from Blanding; 3 hours from trailhead.

Estimated height: 50 ft.

Map and trail guide: Snow Flat Spring Cave (shown); CUWI p.172–173, DAUT p.262–266, KLCA p.126–127.

Comments: The last 5 miles are unpaved and may require 4WD. This hike is much more difficult than the guidebooks make it sound. This is the second of three waterfalls mentioned in the guidebooks and shown on the topo (which you'll definitely want to take with you). The other two were not flowing when we were there. The third waterfall (dryfall) is about 30 minutes further downstream from the second. Some of our group went on to Neville's Arch so that altogether we were on the trail almost ten hours.

Other waterfalls of the area. There are falls in Salt Creek in Canyonlands National Park: a cascade in the upper reaches, Upper Jump, and Lower Jump; see Adkison (ADUT p.241–244 and 247–248) and Kelsey (KLHC p.244–245, 247–248, 261, 264, 268, 272–273). Cunningham and Burke mention waterfalls in Slickhorn Canyon (CUWI p.174–175), accessed by floating the San Juan River, and in Harts Spring Canyon (CUWI p.222–224). Day (DAUT p.224–228) mentions waterfalls in Dark Canyon and at the mouth of its subsidiary, Youngs Canyon. Kelsey (KLHC) mentions waterfalls in Spring Canyon (p.119, 128), Musselman Canyon (p.203–204), and Little Spring Canyon (p.245, 248). Kelsey (KLCA) mentions waterfalls in Courthouse Wash (p.60–61), Bowdie Canyon (p.108–109), Gypsum Canyon (p.108–109), Hammond Canyon (p.120–121, 319), and Water Canyon in The Maze (p.78–79). Tilton mentions a waterfall in Fable Valley (TIUT p.272–273). The GNIS lists The Thumb Pouroff, but this appears to be a dryfall. There are small waterfalls in Negro Bill Canyon north of Moab. There is a small, attractive waterfall along Shafer Creek in the La Sal Mountains. A trail description is in Canyon Country's La Sal Mountains, by Jose Knighton, p.66.

More Waterfalls

Following is a sample of what is coming in the second volume of Utah Waterfalls.

Central Utah

Gordon Creek upstream waterfall (Pinnacle Peak)

Directions: From exit 261 of I-15 drive southeast 62 miles to Consumers Road on the north end of Price (between milepost 235 and 236). Drive west on Consumers Road for 2.6 miles to where a dirt road (which may be gated) turns south just before the large coal loading plant by the railroad line. You should have a high clearance vehicle, dry weather, and the Pinnacle Peak 7.5" topo to drive this road. Follow the road for 2.4 miles until it crosses the railroad tracks. There are minor side roads but the main road is easy to follow. Continue another 0.9 miles past the railroad tracks to where a couple of side roads (marked as a jeep trail on the map) turn off to the right. This side road continues to the top of the falls, but is not recommended since it has a steep sandy section

and a rock ledge that could be dangerous. It's only about one mile to the falls from here, so it's just as easy to walk.

Trail description: Hike west on the jeep road down into the North Fork of Gordon Creek (10 min.), across the creek and up the other side and along the bench above the South Fork of Gordon Creek. It's about 25 minutes to a first view of the falls and another 5 minutes on down the road to the top of the falls. The best view of the full falls is back downstream along the bank.

Distances: 117 mi. from SLC; 14 mi. from Price; 30 min. from trailhead, or 2 hours from trailhead without high clearance.

Estimated height: 80 ft.

Map and trail guide: Pinnacle Peak (shown); BRMO p.208–211.

Comments: There is no trail to the foot of the falls and probably no point in trying to get there, since the views from the bank are close enough to get the full effect of the double drop. The last 3 miles to the trailhead are unpaved and unsuitable for passenger cars. This waterfall is so beautiful and so easy to reach that it would be worth hiking or biking from Consumers Road if you don't have a high clearance vehicle — although it's out in the sun. You may want wading boots to cross the North Fork; the topo map shows it as a seasonal stream, but when we were there in late May we found it about a foot deep and too wide to jump across.

South Central Utah

Moss Falls [Bear Canyon] (Mt. Catherine)

Directions: From exit 167 of I-15 drive south 2 miles to the center of Fillmore. Turn east onto 200 South (aka Canyon Road) and drive 9.5 miles to the Pistol Rock Picnic Area. Park a little ways past here in the parking area where the road switchbacks uphill. The trailhead sign for Bear Canyon-Pine Creek Trail can be seen just across the road.

Trail description: Make up your mind to get wet feet if you hike this trail. There are seven stream crossings; the stream is broad and almost knee deep, so old boots that can be used for wading are recommended. Head up the trail (an old road) for about a minute to an old fence. Although a path is worn along the fence, the actual trail goes downhill at this point and crosses the stream obliquely; look upstream a ways to see where it emerges again on the other side. As you continue on the trail there are four more stream crossings in the next 20 minutes. About 5 minutes past the 5th crossing you should reach the well-signed junction with the Cedar Springs Trail; continue to the right on Trail #4021 toward Paradise Canyon. In another 10 minutes the trail crosses the stream again, climbs a couple of switchbacks, and continues upstream well above the stream level. In another 20 minutes you should reach the Three Forks junction; continue to the right on Trail #3521 toward Paradise Canyon. In less than 10 minutes you will come to the 7th crossing. The trail passes a series of nice cascades in about 10 minutes, and then climbs steeply for another 10 minutes to an opening in the trees where Moss Falls can be seen pouring out of the forest and around two sides of a large rock across the canyon from the trail. There are several good viewpoints along the trail, but no trail down the steep canyon walls to the foot of the falls.

Distance: 155 mi. from SLC; 10 mi. from Fillmore; 85 min. from trailhead.

Estimated height: 100 ft.

Map and trail guide: Mt. Catherine (not shown); BIFI p.111.

Comments: The last 7 miles to the trailhead are unpaved. The road is well graded gravel/dirt, but looks like it would be slippery when wet. A walking stick might be handy when crossing the stream; it's clear, so you can see the shallow spots, but it's also swift and rocky. About 5 minutes before the Falls, a side trail leads downhill to an extensive camp with a picnic table. I tried bushwhacking upstream from here to get to the foot of the falls, but was unsuccessful. The falls seem to be fed by a large spring; there doesn't seem to be a channel from the top of the hill. The name Moss Falls comes from Biddle but seems to be otherwise unknown; none of the federal offices in Fillmore had heard of the falls or could tell me its location.

Southeast Utah

Horse Creek upper waterfall [La Sal Mtns.] (Mt. Tukuhnikivatz)

Directions: From exit 180 of I-70, drive south 39 miles on Highway 191, through Moab to the turnoff to the La Sal Mts. Loop Road (County Road 126) at milepost 118. Turn left (east) for half a mile, then right. Continue to follow the signs for the Loop Road as it winds up into the mountains. About 11.5 miles from Highway 191, County Road 126 turns right toward Geyser Pass; continue straight on the Loop Road. In another half mile the road crosses Horse Creek (signed) and about ¾ mile further it reaches the turnoff to Oowah Lake. About half way between Horse Creek and the Oowah Lake Road, look for a wide spot where you can pull off the road.

Trail description: Walk along the road, looking for a tall pine tree near which there is a clearing in the underbrush on the hillside below the road. Go down through this open area to the cliffs along Horse Creek, aiming a short ways upstream to where, from one spot on a cliff that juts out above Horse Creek, you can see this double falls in the creek just upstream.

Distances: 251 mi. from SLC; 21 mi. from Moab; 5–10 min. from parking spot.

Estimated height: 25 ft. (upper half) + 15 ft. (lower half).

Map and trail guide: Mount Tukuhnikivatz; found by serendipity, at the suggestion of Jose Knighton.

Comments: All roads are paved to the trailhead, except the short section after the road crosses Horse Creek. There is no trail to the viewpoint, but the bushwhacking is not difficult. Try to switchback across the hillside when hiking downhill, to avoid eroding the terrain.

Indian Creek waterfall (North Six-shooter Peak)

Directions: From exit 180 of I-70, drive south 71 miles on Highway 191 to Highway 211 (between milepost

86 and 87) leading to the Needles section of Canyonlands National Park. Turn right (west) and drive 20 miles to the official end of Highway 211. The road continues toward the park; continue another 10 miles to the signed junction with the Lockhart Basin Road. Turn right (north) on this road and continue 3 miles, past a couple of campsites with picnic tables, to where the road fords Indian Creek. Park here.

Trail description: Walk over to the creek and along it for a short ways downstream for a view of the waterfall.

Distances: 303 miles from SLC; 48 mi. from Monticello; 1 min. from parking spot.

Estimated height: 10 ft. + 10 ft. of cascades in upper section.

Map and trail guide: North Six-shooter Peak: information from the Needles Outpost.

Comments: The last 3 miles, on the Lockhart Basin Road, are unpaved, but it's a good road, generally passable by passenger cars.

Appendix: Top Ten Lists

Author's Top Ten Favorite Waterfalls

1. Fifth Water upper waterfall
2. Lower Calf Creek Falls
3. Singletree Falls
4. Menu Falls
5. Upper Calf Creek Falls
6. Stewart Falls
7. Provo River Falls
8. Adams Canyon lower waterfall
9. Battle Creek Canyon lower waterfall
10. Aspen Grove third waterfall

Top Ten Roadside Waterfalls

1. Provo River Falls upper
2. Bridal Veil Falls
3. Ogden Canyon waterfall
4. Chicken Creek waterfall
5. Ford Creek waterfall
6. Alpine Scenic Loop first waterfall
7. Alta City
8. Temple of Sinawava
9. Fremont River waterfall
10. Laurel Pines spring

Top Ten Waterfalls Reached in Less Than Ten Minutes

1. Menu Falls
2. Camp Creek waterfall
3. Hidden Falls
4. Moss Ledge waterfall
5. Provo River Falls middle waterfall
6. Provo River Falls lower waterfall
7. Lake Blanche outlet waterfall

8. The Falls
9. Lisa Falls
10. Milky Falls

Top Ten Waterfalls Reached in Less Than Thirty Minutes

1. Singletree Falls
2. Adams Canyon lower waterfall
3. Blue Spring Creek waterfall
4. Battle Creek Canyon lower waterfall
5. Cascade Falls
6. Kens Lake waterfall
7. Rocky Mouth Canyon waterfall
8. Lower Emerald Pool
9. Battle Creek Canyon second waterfall
10. Mill Creek lower waterfall

Top Ten Waterfalls Reached in Less Than Ninety Minutes

1. Fifth Water upper waterfall
2. Lower Calf Creek Falls
3. Upper Calf Creek Falls
4. Stewart Falls
5. Aspen Grove third waterfall
6. Fifth Water middle waterfall
7. Ely Creek waterfall
8. Aspen Grove second waterfall
9. Bullion Falls
10. Timpooneke Trail fourth waterfall

Bibliography

ADHI Adkison, Ron. *Hiking Grand Staircase-Escalante and the Glen Canyon region*. Falcon, c1998. 346 p.

ADUT Adkison, Ron. *Utah's National Parks: hiking, camping and vacationing in Utah's canyon country. Wilderness Press*, c1991. 354 p.

BESC Bensen, Joe. *Scenic driving Utah*. Falcon Press, c1996. 248 p.

BIFI Biddle, M. *Fishlake National Forest: Back Country Guide for Hiking and Horseback Riding*. Wasatch Publishers, c1993. 122 p.

BOWA Bottcher, Betty, editing, assisted by Mel Davis. *Wasatch trails: Salt Lake City area*. Wasatch Mountain Club, c1973. 77 p.

BREX Brereton, Thomas and James Dunaway. *Exploring the backcountry of Zion National Park: off-trail routes*. Rev. and updated by Bob Lineback. Zion Natural History Association, c1988. 112 p.

BRMO Bromka, Gregg. *Mountain Biker's Guide to Utah*. Falcon Press, c1994. 361 p.

BRUT Brewer, Ted. *Utah off the beaten path*. Globe Pequot Press, c1996. 163 p.

BUAL Burton, D. Jeff and Marlene K. Burton. *Along the Great Western Trail: trails between Parleys and Ogden Canyons near Salt Lake City, Utah: the Wasatch front's other wilderness*. IVE, c1995. 80 p.

CUWI Cunningham, Bill & Polly Burke. *Wild Utah.* Falcon, c1998. 383 p.

DACA Davis, Mel, and Ann Schimpf, editors. *Cache Trails: a hiking guide for trails in the Cache Valley, Utah area.* USU Foundation, c1974. 96 p.

DAUT Day, David. *Utah's Favorite Hiking Trails.* Rincon Publishing Co., c1998. 367 p.

GEWA Geery, Daniel. *Wasatch trails: Salt Lake City area. Volume two.* Wasatch Mountain Club, c1977. 112 p.

HAHI Hall, Dave. *The Hiker's Guide to Utah.* Revised by Ann Seifert. Falcon Press, c1991. 244 p.

HUUT Huegel, Tony. *Utah byways: Backcountry drives for the whole family.* Post Company, c1996. 174 p.

KEBE Keilty, Maureen. *Best Hikes With Children in Utah.* Photos by Dan Peha. The Mountaineers, c1993. 240 p.

KLCA Kelsey, Michael R. *Canyon Hiking Guide to the Colorado Plateau.* 4th ed. Kelsey Publishing, c1999. 320 p.

KLCL Kelsey, Michael R. *Climbing And Exploring Utah's Mt. Timpanogos.* Kelsey Publishing, c1989. 208 p.

KLHC Kelsey, Michael R. *Hiking, Biking and Exploring Canyonlands National Park and Vicinity.* Kelsey Publishing, c1992. 320 p.

KLHP Kelsey, Michael R. *Hiking and Exploring the Paria River*. 3rd ed. Kelsey Publishing, c1998. 224 p.

KLHU Kelsey, Michael R. *Hiking And Exploring Utah's Henry Mountains And Robbers Roost*. Kelsey Publishing, c1987. 224 p.

LAHI Lambrechtse, Rudi. *Hiking the Escalante*. Wasatch Publishers, c1985. 192 p.

LIHI Lineback, Bob. *Hiking in Zion National Park: the trails*. Zion Natural History Association, c1988. 48 p.

MANA Magley, Beverly. *National Forest scenic byways*. Falcon Press, c1990. 240 p.

MANF Magley, Beverly. *National Forest scenic byways II*. Falcon Press, c1992. 210 p.

MOHI Molvar, Erik & Tomara Martin. *Hiking Zion & Bryce Canyon National Parks*. Falcon, c1997. 245 p.

NITR Nichols, Gary C. *Trails of the Wasatch: a pocket guide*. Printed by Litho Graphics, c1996. 98 p.

PAUT Paxman, Shirley and Monroe, Gayle and Weldon Taylor. *Utah Valley trails: a hiking guide to the many scenic trails around Provo, Utah*. Wasatch Publishers, c1978. 71 p.

TIUT Tilton, Buck. *Utah hiking: the complete guide to more than 300 of the best hikes in the beehive state*. Foghorn Press, c1999. 314 p.

URTR Urmann, David. *Trail Guide to Grand Staircase Escalante National Monument*. Gibbs-Smith Publisher, c1999. 160 p.

VEHI Veranth, John. *Hiking the Wasatch: a hiking and natural history guide to the central Wasatch*. Wasatch Mountain Club, c1988. 202 p.

WHUT Wharton, Tom. *Utah!: A Family Travel Guide*. Wasatch Publishers, c1987. 224 p.

Photo of author at Sand Creek falls north of Torrey. (To be included in second book.)

Photo credits: Nos. 94, 96 and the photo to the left by Chris Moore; all others by the author.

Index